The Georgia RAMBLER

A POTTER'S SNAKE, THE REAL THING RECIPE, A SATILLA ADVENTURE AND MORE

CHARLES SALTER

Charleston · London

THE History PRESS

Published by The History Press
Charleston, SC 29403
www.historypress.net

Cover design and illustration by Karleigh Hambrick.
All images by the author unless otherwise noted.

First published 2011

Manufactured in the United States

ISBN 978.1.60949.202.1

Library of Congress Cataloging-in-Publication Data
Salter, Charles E.
The Georgia rambler / Charles Salter.
p. cm.
Summary: Collection of columns featuring the most interesting characters
found throughout Georgia; originally appeared in the Atlanta journal and
constitution, 1976 to 1980.
ISBN 978-1-60949-202-1
1. Georgia--Social life and customs--Anecdotes. 2. Georgia--Biography--
Anecdotes. I. Atlanta journal and constitution magazine. II. Title.
F286.6.S25 2011
975.8--dc23
2011019206

To my dear wife, Sallye, who encouraged and inspired me every mile of my journey across the state when I wrote several hundred columns as the Georgia Rambler for the Atlanta Journal *and Sunday's* Atlanta Journal and Constitution.

Contents

Acknowledgements   7
Introduction   9

PART I. DUOS
Love's Flame Survives Civil War   15
Old Moonshine Not Better   19
Moonshiner Needed a Level Head   22
Fiddlin' John Carson and Moonshine Kate   25
A Potter and His Silent Partner   29
Miraculous Survival at Sea   32
Golden Dreams   35
Short, Sweet and Cheap Weddings   38

PART II. LIFE'S WORK
Fightin' Mad   43
J.B., Thunder and the Lord in Fields   48
Adventure on Satilla River   51
Last of the Polite Tobacco Chewers   54
A Garden Dedicated to God   56
Legend about Good Luck   60
Shaving Horse Gives Close Shave   63
Message of Hope, Faith and Love   66
Singer Says Gangster Was Sweet, Courteous   69

CONTENTS

PART III. WAY BACK WHEN

Does Sign of Snake Point to Gold?   75
Everyone Can't Be a King   79
More Than a Fishing Village   82
Living in the Style of the 1800s   85
Sermon Really Shook Them Up   89
Old Houses from Genteel Era   91
Wild Hogs Roamed in Mountains   94

PART IV. EXITS

Destiny Halted Party for FDR   101
Marines Called Oswald the "Creep"   104
Sylvia's Still the Talk of the Town   109
Haunted House Moans and Groans   112
Ghosts Slowly Floated Away   116
Church Booted Straying Members   120
Old Dan Tucker   122
Farewell and Good Luck   125
"Prophet" Prepares for Eternity   127

PART V. SIDE TRIPS

Is It the Coca-Cola Recipe?   133
How Old Coke Became New Coke News   136
Herbs for What Ails You   139
Mysterious Night of the Mull   142
Chief Vann's House   145
Mr. Bass Tells Turtle Tales   149
Teacher Loves Country Music   152
Teller of Tall Swamp Tales   155
Family Life in Okefenokee   158
Country Cooking Fit for a President   161
Memories of a Barefoot Boy   164
Sense of Belonging Gone   167

Index   171
About the Author   175

Acknowledgments

I am very grateful to my newspaper colleagues, friends, acquaintances, fishermen, countless people I met in towns across the state and family members. They all contributed so much to my work as the Atlanta newspapers' "Georgia Rambler" and made the column a memorable and happy experience.

Durwood "Mac" McAlister, the managing editor of the *Atlanta Journal*, promoted me from picture editor to state news editor, which led to the column. Jim Minter, the next managing editor, and city editor Herb Steely both were supportive, as was news editor Paul Howle, who gave my columns and photos good display in the paper. Photo department manager Marion Johnson and his staff taught me a great deal about 35mm cameras and various lenses, which was useful since I photographed the subjects myself after my interviews.

I was fortunate to have excellent sources, people I had met through my fishing columns and features who suggested column ideas. Charles Cunningham, the postmaster in Madison, and Everett Beal, a pharmacist in Griffin and Gainesville, were especially helpful. I also turned to Jack Wingate, fishing camp operator on Lake Seminole; Tommy Shaw, a marina owner on Clarks Hill reservoir; Willie Allen, marina owner on Lake Jackson; state fisheries biologists Russ England and Reggie Weaver, both in Gainesville, and Wayne Thomaston in Macon; and Eddie Withrow of Lula, Georgia, a bus driver and Atlanta fishing tackle salesman. And in many of the communities, there were county extension agents, merchants and other residents who steered me in the right direction for interviews with interesting, colorful folks time and again.

ACKNOWLEDGEMENTS

Special thanks to Ira Glass, the host and executive producer of *This American Life*, and his staff for their fine "Georgia Rambler" show in 2010 (available at www.thisamericanlife.org, episode No. 413). Producer Lisa Pollak, my daughter-in-law, took an interest in my old column and told the staff about it. My son, Chuck, a senior writer with *Fast Company* magazine, was one of the Ramblers on the show. He helped me a great deal in preparation of this manuscript.

I'm so grateful that Jessica Berzon, an editor at The History Press, listened to the episode and contacted me about publishing a collection of my columns.

Cathy King, executive director, and Connie New, assistant director, of the historic McDaniel-Tichenor House in Monroe were gracious enough to allow me to photograph paintings of a former governor and his wife to include in this book. And I'm still appreciative after all these years that Anita Sams of Monroe graciously permitted me to quote from the couple's Civil War love letters in her book *With Unabated Trust*.

Introduction

I really did ramble. The "Georgia Rambler" wasn't just the name of my column from 1976 to 1980 in the *Atlanta Journal*. It was an accurate job description as well. If I hadn't arranged an interview ahead of time, I'd pull out a Georgia map first thing in the morning, survey the biggest state east of the Mississippi River and pick a town.

"Where are you going today?" my wife, Sallye, would ask.

"I think I'll head east, maybe to Madison or Greensboro," I'd say. "But I'll be home for supper."

And off I went, headed to places throughout the state where I sometimes didn't know a living soul. But I had grown up in small towns in Georgia. I'd visited them as a lifelong fisherman. And I'd always enjoyed getting to know people. I knew I'd find somebody worth writing about.

I met a farmer and his son in Elbert County fighting to prevent their land from being turned into a new lake. I met an ex-moonshiner in North Georgia and the retired revenue agent he'd eluded for years. I met a Warner Robins woman who had watched a young, intense Lee Harvey Oswald training on a U.S. Marine Corps rifle range. I met two elderly sisters in Jackson who lived and dressed as though it were the 1840s. And one day at a pharmacy in Gainesville, I discovered what might be one of the original recipes for Coca-Cola, which became international news in 2011 (see page 136).

The "Rambler" column grew out of an assignment I got from Durwood McAlister, the managing editor of the *Journal*, to be a roving state news editor. Get out of Atlanta, he told me. Find out what's happening elsewhere in the state. At the time, I was writing a twice-weekly column about fishing, and I welcomed the chance to be on my own, away from a noisy office and the Atlanta traffic.

It didn't take long for me to realize that I was drawn more to the people in those towns than a deadline news story. I believe that nearly everyone has a good story to tell. It could be about his or her work, family, personal struggles or community.

I modeled myself after Ernie Pyle, a journalist I greatly admire. He was best known for his World War II columns, when he chronicled the lives of enlisted American soldiers on the front lines in Europe and the Pacific. I had also enjoyed his earlier work, the "Home Country" columns about everyday America. In the 1930s, he traveled the country, writing an oral history about ordinary people who don't often get written about.

I took a similar approach in my column, focusing on people throughout Georgia. Men and women. Young and old. Black and white. Those living in the mountains and those on the coast. I wasn't looking for the powerful or the famous—the newsmakers—although I did discover good stories related to then-president Jimmy Carter, John F. Kennedy and FDR. I wanted to capture a way of life that many of the newspaper's readers in Atlanta knew little about. Beyond the suburbs, far from modern city life, there were Georgians who still farmed using a horse-drawn plow instead of a tractor. Who prided themselves on the country cooking handed down from their mamas and grandmamas. Who were aware of history in a way that the new arrivals to Atlanta weren't.

But to find those people, I needed to explore—to ramble. So we called the column "Georgia Rambler." The *Journal* outfitted me with a car, a white station wagon emblazoned on both sides with my name and that of the paper and the column.

I asked people I'd written about or met during my years doing fishing columns for leads. And I just showed up in towns and walked into the local barbershop or country store. "Maybe you've read that *Reader's Digest* article about the 'most unforgettable character' you know," I'd say. "Who fits that description in your town?"

Many of the people I met had never met a newspaperman, much less been interviewed. A few feared a big-city reporter who showed up on their doorstep with a pen, notebook, tape recorder and 35mm camera. Some wondered what I was after and worried I was going to poke fun at them. I had to win their trust. It helped immensely that I had grown up in small towns myself. I was born in Ocilla and then grew up in Greensboro, Athens and Waycross.

Most weeks, I was on the road two days doing interviews and in the newsroom transcribing and writing for three days. I produced as many as five "Georgia Rambler" columns a week, in addition to two fishing columns. It was the most prolific period in my newspaper career, and I still wonder how I pulled it off. By the time the assignment ended in 1980, I had written more than five hundred "Georgia Rambler" columns. I retired from the *Journal* in 1998.

I was surprised and happy to see the "Georgia Rambler" make a comeback in 2010. The public radio show *This American Life* broadcast an hour-long show inspired by the column. Several reporters traveled to Georgia to be modern-day Ramblers, and host Ira Glass interviewed me about my experience. My son, Chuck, a senior writer at *Fast Company* magazine, was one of the Ramblers on the show. He also helped me put this collection together.

Revisiting my columns after thirty-one years, I feel fortunate to have found so many unforgettable people who allowed me, a total stranger, into their lives and let me share what we talked about in the newspaper. I knew that I was chronicling a vanishing part of Georgia history, a slower and simpler time, and preserving some distinctive voices. Many of the people I wrote about are long gone, and the winds of change have swept through those small towns. But I like to think the tradition continues, that the people living there take the time to tell their children and the occasional curious out-of-towner about the good old days and the history of their community.

I hope you'll find these stories as interesting and memorable as I did when I rambled across Georgia.

Part I
Duos

Love's Flame Survives Civil War

MONROE—A young Confederate army officer went away to war in 1861 with a great sense of patriotism about the South's "cause" and a deep love for his slender, brown-haired sweetheart back home in Monroe.

Henry McDaniel feared at times during the next four years that he would never live to see Hester Felker again. He fervently hoped and prayed she would wait for him to return home after the long, bloody Civil War. McDaniel was seriously wounded shortly after the battle at Gettysburg, captured by Northern troops and imprisoned in Maryland and later in Ohio. The letters that he wrote her during those four years not only are a tender, beautiful love story but also are colorful, quite detailed accounts of historic battles and his associations with some of the famous Confederate leaders.

About ten years ago while doing research for a book on the history of Walton County, Mrs. Anita B. Sams of Monroe learned that these love letters had been discovered in Hester's old bonnet box. Hester had saved only two of her own letters to her future husband. Mrs. Sams received permission of Mrs. Emily Tichenor, widow of McDaniel's grandson, Henry McDaniel Tichenor, and Mrs. Frances Warfield, Tichenor's sister, for the letters to be published by the Historical Society of Walton County, Inc., in a book, *With Unabated Trust*. The title of Mrs. Sams's book was a phrase used by McDaniel in one of the wartime love letters.

Henry McDaniel, an 1856 graduate of Mercer Institute at Penfield, practiced law in Monroe before and after the war, and he was governor of Georgia from 1883 to 1886. Construction of the state capitol began during

Henry McDaniel, shown in a painting about 1897, wrote love letters to Hester Felker while he was a prisoner in the North during the Civil War. He hoped and prayed she would wait for him to return home. *Courtesy of McDaniel-Tichenor House Inc.*

his administration. His father, Ira McDaniel, built one of Atlanta's first brick stores around 1847.

Henry was twenty-one and Hester seventeen when they met in 1857 at the Female Academy. Six years later in the siege of Suffolk, he was to write her, "Retrospect is always sad, more or less. I would give so much to live that evening over again."

Because her father disapproved of the courtship, he had to send his wartime letters to Hester's brother-in-law and half sister, who delivered them to her.

McDaniel's first letter in *With Unabated Trust* refers to the 1861 Milledgeville convention, where, as a delegate of twenty-four, he "doubted the wisdom of secession" but voted for it on the final ballot when passage was certain.

From Camp Bartow at Manassas, Virginia, later in 1861, McDaniel wrote, "Scarce a day has passed for two or three weeks that three volleys of musketry have not announced the burial of a soldier." He was saddened at the death of General F.S. Bartow, whose final words were, "Boys, they have killed me, but never give up the fight."

At Centreville, Virginia, in November 1861, McDaniel quoted General Robert Tombs as remarking about the Walton County troops: "Those fellows are not as handsomely dressed as the Virginians, but they can shoot like h-ll." From battlefields, McDaniel urged his sweetheart to write longer letters, and more often, and he requested a tress of her hair.

In Virginia, he closed a letter in pencil with this touching thought: "And now, Hester, I commend you to the care of the Good Fairies, who keep tender watch over loving and lovely maidens, beseeching that not a hair of your head shall be visited too roughly by the winds, and not an untoward

Hester Felker McDaniel, in a painting about 1897, kept love letters from Henry McDaniel in her bonnet box. Their letters were in a book by Anita Sams, *With Unabated Trust*, published by the Historical Society of Walton County Inc. *Courtesy of McDaniel-Tichenor House Inc.*

circumstance may mar your pleasures."

McDaniel, who was to rise to the rank of major before his two-year imprisonment, reminisced about his fondness for eggnog but declared, "I think the Yankees never had refinement enough to eat it. Think of a Yankee eating eggnog. The gods would interfere to prevent such a sacrilege. It would be as bad as if the rascals should attempt to accustom themselves to corn field peas in the hope of becoming respectable people."

In his letters, McDaniel was the ardent lover, expressing his deep feelings for Hester, but she was reserved and cool, as was the custom of ladies of that day. He wrote, "Too strict maidenly reserve is very chilling to a lover, as well as unjust." In 1872, several years after their marriage, however, she was to write while he was away on business, "I depend upon you for everything, for every pleasure as well as comfort of my life. You may be well aware that you have me completely in your own hands."

Near Richmond in May 1862, McDaniel wrote, "Sometimes we live on hard bread and fat bacon, sometimes eaten raw, at other times broiled on sticks."

When General T.R.R. Cobb was killed at Fredericksburg in 1862, McDaniel said he "admired him more, perhaps, than any other son of my state."

He referred to his sleeping under the stars of Virginia and awakening and wondering which star guarded Hester, which was her favorite and whether they gazed at the same star at the same time.

In March 1863, he saw Confederate president Jefferson Davis in a Richmond church service, describing him as "careworn and jaded...I thought of the tremendous burdens resting upon his shoulders, apparently so feeble."

Henry McDaniel, a major in the Confederate army, was wounded while retreating with his troops after the Battle of Gettysburg. He thought wistfully of his sweetheart when he was taken from the field. *Courtesy of McDaniel-Tichenor House Inc.*

In another letter in 1863, McDaniel described the Southern soldiers' famous yell in battle. "There is nothing on earth like the cheering of our boys in battle," he said. "It is as unlike that of the enemy as two modes of doing the same thing could be. The enemy's 'Huzza' Huzza' Huzza' is made three times and in concert. Ours consists of a series of independent yells, each man yelling for himself and yelling until the front is gained. We can always tell in battle when our boys are driving the enemy."

McDaniel suffered a stomach wound on July 10, 1863, after retreating with his troops following the battle at Gettysburg, and two days later he was captured by Yankee soldiers at Hagerstown, Maryland. Six weeks after being shot, he wrote Hester, "When I was stricken down and borne from the field, I thought wistfully of you." He was taken to a hospital in Point Lookout, Maryland, and later transferred to Johnson's Island at Sandusky, Ohio.

In the spring of 1864, McDaniel was saddened to learn his invalid mother had died in Georgia and that his brother Sanders was killed in a battle and his younger brother Ira was wounded.

General Robert E. Lee and his men surrendered on April 9, 1865, at the Appomattox Courthouse, but it was not until July 25 that Henry McDaniel finally was freed from prison. In one of his last letters from prison, McDaniel said his separation from Hester "has been long and cruel. It has seemed to me sometimes that the dark cloud so long overshadowing us would never be lifted."

Henry McDaniel and Hester Felker were wed on December 20, 1865, in Monroe, and had one son and one daughter in a happy marriage that was to last sixty years. He died two months before his ninetieth birthday in 1926, and she was eighty-nine when she passed away in 1929.

Old Moonshine Not Better

JASPER—Don't believe those folks in the mountains who claim that moonshine made in the 1920s and 1930s was far better than the white lightning of today, says a retired "revenooer." Duff Floyd, seventy-six, of Jasper, who spent thirty-five years destroying illegal distilleries and arresting moonshiners, says, "It was poor quality then, too."

During his career, he met only two men, both residents of Gilmer County, who made pure corn whiskey. "They couldn't compete," he said. "They made it for their own use and for special friends and got a fancy prize for it." Pure corn whiskey required about nine days to make, but the typical moonshiner ran off his less desirable kind of booze in just three or four days.

Floyd said it was very common to find dead animals floating in fermenters deep in the woods of mountain counties. "Possums would climb over the box and get in the fermenters and drown," he recalled. "He might be in there several days. I have even seen dead skunks in fermenters. They'd get a pitchfork, drop it off on the ground and cook it off. In South Georgia, they buried the fermenters in the ground sometimes, and occasionally hogs would get in there and drown. Quality moonshine was very rare indeed."

The retired revenue agent, whose career began in 1929 during Prohibition, never drinks alcoholic beverages. "It would cure anybody to see what moonshiners did."

Making moonshine was a way of life that had been taught from one generation to the next in the mountains, and Floyd learned early in his career that "there were plenty of fellows raised in it who would tell you the truth about anything."

Retired revenue agent Duff Floyd spent thirty-five years destroying illegal distilleries and arresting moonshiners in the North Georgia mountains. He sometimes found dead possums and skunks floating in fermenters deep in the woods.

He remembers a conversation with a former moonshiner beside a mailbox on a dirt road one day during the Depression. Floyd had just let some agents out of his car to hunt a moonshine still in the woods, and he saw an old man walk out of a house to pick up the mail. He said the still being hunted probably was operated by the old-timer's sons.

"I stopped to pass the time of day, and he got to talking," said Floyd. "He said, 'Yes, Floyd, I have made a lot of liquor and sold it. I got too old, and I haven't made liquor in years.'"

The old-timer told Floyd he had made liquor not to violate the law but because "about the only thing we had in the way of a cash crop was, occasionally, you could sell a few crossties. We had no schools worth anything, no good roads, no form of communication with the outside world."

When he made moonshine, the old man had several young children either in school or nearing the age to enroll. Floyd continued, "He told me, 'I'd go down to Ellijay and see other children walkin' the streets with an armful of books (not free at that time), good clothes on, good shoes on, and my children barefooted. I had no way to get anything.

"I wanted my children to have an education, have some good shoes and clothes to wear. I didn't have anything else I could get money out of except make some liquor and sell it. That's why I made moonshine."

Floyd, a tall, slender native of Bartow County, never had to fire his revolver as a revenue agent, and he was so familiar with his territories over the years that he usually recognized the moonshiners when he arrived at their stills. "In the territory I knew, the people I knew, I wouldn't have cared if I had gone in there without even a pocketknife," he said. "No, I wasn't afraid. If they got a chance, they ran and we had to catch them. Usually they wouldn't resist. Lots of times they didn't see me, and I'd be in there talkin' to them before they knew it. I'd walk up and say, 'Are you boys makin' pretty good stuff?'"

One day, Floyd and agent Wallace Wheeler worked their way around to opposite ends of a big steamer distillery while a moonshiner was telling his pal about his escapade with a local woman. Floyd quietly eased into the clearing, squatted down next to a tree and locked his hands around his knees. He recognized both men and knew their names.

One of the men turned and saw Floyd, who smiled and shook his head. The moonshiner, disgusted, asked his partner, "Look around and see if you know this fellow."

The other moonshiner, quite startled when he saw Floyd, muttered, "Hell, no, never saw him before in my life."

Wheeler walked up and assisted Floyd in the arrests.

"With the local people, there was no trouble," said Floyd. He recalled the time that one of his friends, a man of slight build, arrested a six-foot, five-inch moonshiner—a convicted killer who had escaped from an Alabama prison. The escapee had vowed never to be taken alive. The prisoner walked ahead of the short agent on a log across a creek and then suddenly turned, threw him in the water and grabbed for the revolver. In their struggle for the gun, the prisoner twisted it, almost cutting the agent's trigger finger, but the officer was able to squeeze off one round, and the bullet struck the escaped convict's heart, killing him instantly.

Moonshiner Needed a Level Head

CARTERSVILLE—Hubert Howell says he made moonshine for about fifteen years beside creeks in hollows and woods of North Georgia, but the "revenooers" never caught him. Many of his pals and neighbors weren't as fortunate.

Howell, seventy-nine, whose main interest nowadays is growing vegetables at his rural home on Georgia 20, three miles east of Cartersville, chuckled as he explained why he never spent a day or night in jail. "I didn't smoke, and I didn't drink," he said. "That was the secret of them not catchin' me. If a fellow got drunk, he wasn't no trouble catchin'. It was made to sell, not to drink. I always said a man was a damned fool for drinkin'. Drinkin' was a mistake. Sho' was. You're not levelheaded when you're drinkin'. You think you know more than the officers do. You get cocky."

Howell, who hasn't made moonshine since he donned an army uniform in 1942 during World War II, boasts that he once was faster than a rabbit. "There wasn't nothin' with two legs that could outrun me," he said. "And I've run down many a rabbit. I was pickin' cotton in a field, and I'd throw off my pick sack and chase him."

One autumn day in the 1930s, he had to run four miles through a Cherokee County forest to escape from a puffing, determined revenue agent.

Howell, born in a one-room log cabin on Stamp Creek, now part of Lake Allatoona, claimed that on more than one occasion, he eluded federal revenue agent Duff Floyd, who became a legendary figure destroying moonshine stills for thirty-five years. "Duff Floyd couldn't catch me," said Howell, grinning. "He raided lots of my stills. The revenooers was in every week. It was hard to make it."

Hubert Howell examines ruins of a moonshine still raided many years earlier by revenue agents in the mountains. He made moonshine before World War II and said he was never caught by lawmen because he stayed sober and kept a level head.

He remembers sprinting to freedom moments before Floyd and other agents dynamited a moonshine still and found some of his hogs feeding in the area. "I had the awfulest bunch of hogs up there you ever tell of," said Howell. "So, Duff Floyd come up to my house and said, 'Hubert, some of the biggest hogs I ever saw are down at the old still house. We cut it down.'

"And, he said, 'You better get them up. I know they belong to you.' I said, 'I'll see if they're mine. Other people have hogs up here, too.'

The revenue agent added, 'They're too valuable to be out like that.'"

Howell laughed and added, "They were big hogs. I fed 'em on beer rations. Duff's a good man. We respected the revenooers. They weren't like them tin can officers in town. They treated us like gentlemen."

Howell said he made liquor over a period of several years in the 1930s for John Henry Hardin, a prosperous Cherokee County farmer who was described as being the king of Georgia moonshiners. "I made moonshine many a day for John Henry Hardin," said Howell. "I worked by the hour and by the gallon. I used to make a dollar an hour."

Howell remembers that Hardin had several moonshine stills in operation at the same time and "could'a made one thousand gallons a day in one place" but knew it was too great a risk. "He didn't go down there unless it was a big still," said Howell. "Sometimes eight men worked at one still. It took four men to gather wood and four to take care of the still."

Revenue agents worked for years trying to catch Hardin at a still but only were able to gather evidence to convict him on conspiracy charges.

Referring again to his own numerous escapes, Howell said he and his colleagues were constantly on the alert for agents approaching the still in a hollow. "I would always figure out how to get away down the hollow," said Howell. "They'd send some pot-gutted fellow to flush you out. I'd walk toward him, he'd stick his hand out to shake hands and I'd go under his hand and be done gone."

Howell claims that agents shot at him fleeing in the woods several times. How did it feel to hear bullets whistling past him? "It helps you along," he said, grinning. "It gives you wings."

Near Laughing Gal, a former community in Cherokee County, thirteen miles west of Canton, Howell and I walked in the woods and jumped across a branch to look at pieces of rusty metal—all that remains of one of his stills that agents dynamited nearly forty years ago.

"We wasn't doin' anything wrong [making moonshine]," Howell said. "We was a-makin' our bread, our livin', by the sweat of our faces. We made it honestly. I never stole anything to make any whiskey with. I always paid good cash for what I bought. People around here didn't look down on us for makin' liquor."

He insisted his moonshine was clean and denied often-told tales about drowned possum and other animals floating in slowly fermenting booze. "That was all just talk to keep you from buyin' it," said Howell. "It's a kind of trade talk put out by fellows who sold government whiskey."

Could he get away with making moonshine in modern times? "If the same thing [hard times] was to come up again, I could," he declared. "I could make it now and get by with it. I know danged well I could. It just takes a level head to do it."

Before retiring from the liquor business and entering the wartime army, Howell considered purchasing a "big, four-story rock castle" in North Georgia for an expanded moonshine distillery. "I was gonna put baby chickens on the first two floors, and the next two floors I was gonna have my distilleries," he said. "I would run all the slop and waste from the stills down to a hog pen and raise hogs. The chickens would have covered the smell of the still. I would have got by with it. Figured I could make one thousand gallons a day. Nobody on earth would'a known about it."

Nobody, perhaps, but Duff Floyd, whose long legs might have caught up with Hubert Howell at last.

But, sitting in the shade of a plum tree next to his Bartow County garden, Howell can dream of what might have been.

Fiddlin' John Carson and Moonshine Kate

DONALSONVILLE—Rosa Lee Johnson's eyes grew misty as she heard recorded sounds of a fiddle and guitar and her late father, Fiddlin' John Carson, singing "Little Log Cabin in the Lane." Her husband, Wayne, played another tape made of records from the 1920s and 1930s, and they listened to Carson sing "The Old Hen Cackled and the Rooster Gonna Crow."

For a few moments, the tape recordings swept away the barrier of time, and Mrs. Johnson, sixty-five, was reliving those rousing years when she performed under the name of Moonshine Kate with her father and his Virginia Reelers on stages from coast to coast.

"Little Log Cabin in the Lane" made her especially nostalgic because it was not only one of this natural-born fiddler's own favorites but also the song he played and sang on WSB radio in March 1922. Her father was the first country musician to appear on the "new-fangled" radio station in Atlanta. WSB was the first radio station that went on the air in the South.

"Every now and then, I still like to get out my old guitar and play some of those old hillbilly songs," she said, smiling, "but I've got a little touch of arthritis in my hands now."

She removed her father's necktie from its place around a violin case and showed a visitor the fiddle that Carson played from age ten until his death at eighty-one in 1949. "His great-grandfather, Allan Carson, brought it over from Ireland many years ago," Mrs. Johnson said. "It was made in Italy in 1773." She believes it possibly was made by the son of the famed Antonio Stradivari.

Fiddlin' John Carson and his daughter, Rosa Lee Carson, whose stage name was Moonshine Kate, appeared on stage in many towns throughout the South in the late 1920s and 1930s. They also performed at political rallies for gubernatorial candidate Eugene Talmadge. *Courtesy of Country Music Hall of Fame and Museum.*

Although she was born in Atlanta, Mrs. Johnson says she's been a hillbilly—not a city girl—all her life. At the age of three, she sang and danced on a Smyrna school stage and learned to play a guitar and banjo at fourteen, joining her father in show business two years later.

Carson, a native of Cobb County, won fourteen consecutive championships in fiddlers' conventions in Atlanta's old city auditorium, his daughter said. He performed in many states and also in Cuba, Canada and Mexico. "I enjoyed every minute of it," said Mrs. Johnson. "Some places we'd stay just one night, then go to another town. In one town, we performed for three months. We'd rest up at home, then get our clothes ready and leave out again on the road."

A record company decided she needed a stage name, and someone suggested Moonshine Kate after the fiddler recorded "Corn Liquor Still in Georgia." In that record, Moonshine Kate refuses to tell the "revenooers" the location of her pa's whisky still, even though they offer her five dollars, and she warns them, "You sure ain't comin' back."

Moonshine Kate is perhaps best remembered for her very sad rendition of "Little Mary Phagan," the song that Fiddlin' John Carson wrote about a famous Atlanta murder. Leo Frank was accused of the slaying and was lynched in Marietta. "Dad sat right under that tree and composed that song, gave it to me and I recorded it," said Mrs. Johnson. "He also wrote a song about Floyd Collins [a pioneering cave explorer who died in a Kentucky cave in 1925] after he was trapped in a cave."

Duos

Carson is remembered by many Georgians for his regular performances during the political campaigns of the late Gene Talmadge in the 1930s and 1940s. He also fiddled to attract votes for Herman Talmadge, Ed Rivers and Roy Harris. "We'd go from town to town with Gene Talmadge, and he would have a big truck for us to get up there and make music," said Mrs. Johnson. "We'd sing and I'd buck-and-wing dance, and Pa would tell a few jokes in the courthouse square."

When Gene Talmadge cut the price of auto tags, Carson wrote a song called "Georgia's $3 Tag," and he also composed "The Talmadge Special" and "The Talmadge Highball." Mrs. Johnson said, "One of the songs Papa composed about Gene went like this: 'I've got a Eugene dog, I've got a Eugene cat, I'm a Talmadge man from my shoes to my hat.'"

Georgians also heard Carson sing hillbilly songs such as "It's a Shame to Whip Your Wife on Sunday," "Smoke Goes Out the Chimney Just the Same," "There's a Hard Time a Comin'," "I'm Glad My Wife's in Europe," "Don't Let Your Deal Go Down" and "Whatcha Gonna Do When Your Liquor Gives Out?"

Mrs. Johnson regrets that hillbilly music has taken a back seat to country and western selections in recent years, and she doesn't care much for the so-called "Nashville sound." She says most of the country stars aren't hillbillies. "Grandpa Jones is an old hillbilly," she said. "In a way, Roy Clark can play pretty good like they did in hillbilly music. Roy has got a little country in him. I like Loretta Lynn. She is good. She's country, like myself. Her one record that I really love is 'I'm Just a Country Girl.'"

Mrs. Johnson feels that hillbilly music might make a comeback in the wake of country music's growing wave of popularity.

"When I was appearing with Dad, tickets sold for twenty-five cents," she said, "and if the house was packed, we'd bring home fifty to sixty dollars."

One rainy day in the early 1930s, the Carsons' car bogged down in the mud about twelve miles from Franklin, North Carolina, where they were scheduled to perform that night. A farmer brought his mule to the road, but it was unable to pull out the car.

"Pa said, 'Honey, you feel like walkin'?'" Mrs. Johnson said. "I said yes, and he said, 'Get your music and we'll walk down the railroad.' We got a man to watch the car. We walked on the railroad tracks to Franklin, and after the show a gang of 'em walked back up the railroad that night with us. I had my guitar in my hand, and Pa had his fiddle in his hand."

In his later years, Carson was chosen as the official fiddler of the Georgia House of Representatives, and he served as the "elevator commissioner" in the capitol and also as house doorkeeper.

Fiddlin' John Carson and Moonshine Kate were two of the first country music stars ever to make records of their songs. They also performed on radio station WSB shortly after it began broadcasting in Atlanta. *Courtesy of Country Music Hall of Fame and Museum.*

Someone asked Carson how he learned to play the fiddle, and he replied, "Nobody ever showed me anything about it. It was just a natural gift from the Lord. I'm proud I didn't take no lessons. They make fiddlers every day now, but I'm a natural-born fiddler."

Mrs. Johnson said hillbilly music in her fiddling father's time was "music you get out of the mountains—that's where it was taught from."

Neither she nor her father could read music, but both were quite skilled at playing by ear their fiddle, guitar and banjo, and they didn't have difficulty remembering the words to the many hillbilly songs long before television introduced "idiot cards."

Mrs. Johnson retired after working thirty-one years for the City of Atlanta's recreation department, and her husband, Wayne, worked thirty-eight years for an Atlanta business. Their home is about twenty miles south of Donalsonville and just a short drive from the Spring Creek arm of Lake Seminole, where Wayne is a fishing guide.

A Potter and His Silent Partner

MOSSY CREEK—Lanier Meaders prefers to work alone when he shapes a variety of pieces of pottery in a weathered old building across the road from his mountain home. Actually, he has a silent partner who shows up five or six days a week, if the mood strikes him, but the rascal never has been put on the payroll.

His name is Homer. He doesn't hit a lick of work. He just watches Meaders with an apparent glint of approval in his eyes when the pottery is removed from the big kiln.

Homer is a long black snake with a fairly pleasant personality, as reptiles go.

"That snake's in here most days," said Meaders, sixty-one, a third-generation potter. "Homer crawls up and sits there on the shelf and looks at me. He'll stay up there half a day at a time. Homer's agreeable, but he doesn't say anything. He's a lot quieter than a lot of people. Some of 'em talk too much. They really do."

Meaders, whose grandfather, John Meaders, began making pottery in the Mossy Creek community of White County around 1893, said he can't work with anybody around him, bothering him and asking foolish questions. (Especially curious chaps like newspaper reporters?)

He chuckled and made it clear that company was welcome. After unloading pine limbs and logs from a truck in preparation for firing up his kiln, he was ready for a break.

"Pottery is something you have to put all your time in," said Meaders. "Once you let your mind wander just an instant, boy, you've done fouled up."

Lanier Meaders displays pieces of his popular pottery in a weathered building at Mossy Creek, where his silent partner, a fairly pleasant black snake named Homer, sometimes watches for hours from a shelf.

Meaders obviously is a perfectionist, taking pride in every piece of pottery he shapes in the building on Georgia 75, about three miles south of Cleveland in White County. His beautiful works in pottery have been filmed by the Smithsonian Institution and educational television crews.

His batting average "runs about 98 percent," he said, but like every other worker on earth, he does have an occasional day when he's sort of out of rhythm. "Some days I come in here and can't do nothin'," he said, shaking his head. "Nothin' goes right, and when that happens I just get out and leave. The moon? I don't know whether it's the moon or me. It's something. I know that."

I know what he's talking about. Some days I don't set the hook hard enough, and a largemouth bass throws the lure back toward me like a baseball pitcher's curveball.

Meaders served in the 101st Airborne Division in World War II, landing in a glider in the D-Day invasion. Months later, his unit was surrounded by the Germans in a battle that earned the 101st the nickname "the battered bastards of Bastogne." He said, "I'd like to take a trip back to France and other countries and see what it looks like now."

Meaders still is quite a rugged individual, although life is very quiet nowadays, and he works a six-day week despite three heart attacks that likely would have left a city dweller bedridden. "The first one didn't even bother me, and I didn't slow down," he said. "I thought it was indigestion. The next one was a little worse, and it made me sweat a little bit, and I slowed down a couple of days. But, boy, when that next one went, I didn't go no place. It took me five years before I could ever get where I could think straight again."

Unnecessary exertion is strictly taboo, he explained, and I couldn't help but laugh, remembering he had just unloaded a truck filled with pine limbs.

"If I see a rattlesnake on the floor, I would just step over him," said Meaders. "I wouldn't even move him."

Homer probably wouldn't approve of another silent partner crawling into the shop. I must have appeared surprised because he added, "We call it a pilot snake or copperhead. They're just as poisonous as a rattler. A lot more vicious, too. No warning. A rattlesnake—he'll give you a little warning. He's kind of a lazy like thing. If you ever hear him sound off, you'd better jump."

What does a potter do after a long day at the kiln?

"I go to see my girl," said Meaders, smiling.

Miraculous Survival at Sea

DARIEN—Everett "Greek" Gale, a shrimp boat captain for nearly three decades, sat at the dining room table in his two-story, 148-year-old house in historic Darien. His strong hands held a small, framed painting of Jesus walking on the water. He raised the picture to his lips and tenderly kissed it.

"A million dollars wouldn't buy this painting of Jesus," he said. "I bought it for a dollar, maybe less, years ago when a kid knocked on my door selling these paintings to raise money for a church."

Inhaling his cigarette smoke deeply, he sighed, shook his head and declared, "This painting means a lot to me. It was still tacked to the wall in the pilot house four days after that tornado turned my shrimp boat completely over." Gale considers it nothing short of a miracle that he and his son, Frankie, survived the tornado on July 4, 1961.

Two hours before dawn on that memorable day, a shrimp boat owned by his brother, Dave Gale, had been destroyed by fire on a railway, where it had been undergoing routine repairs at the Darien docks. Numerous squalls hit the Georgia coast during the day, and by 6:00 p.m., Greek Gale's forty-two-foot boat, the *Ella D*, and several other fishing vessels were anchored off Little St. Simons Island.

In the galley, Frankie was putting Mercurochrome on his toe that had been cut by barnacles on pilings, while his father, wearing only shorts after his bath, was in the pilothouse.

"I heard this fuss, and it didn't sound right," said Gale. "I told Frankie, 'Somethin's fixin' to happen.' The boat kind of rocked over, and I looked

Everett "Greek" Gale, standing on the docks at Darien. He and his son escaped from his overturned shrimp boat in a tornado. A small, framed picture of Jesus walking on water was found still hanging undamaged on the wall of the pilothouse.

out the window. All I could see was a bunch of gray foam. The whole world had turned to dark, bouncy, gray, pure foam flyin' over the water, like a million tons of soapsuds were flyin' through the air. Never had seen that before."

Seconds later, the powerful wind picked up the shrimp boat as if it were a mere toy and flipped it over, leaving only the keel sticking above the water surface and the mast pointing toward the bottom of the sea.

"Next thing I seen was all water," said Gale. "Just like that—bang, bang. The boat next to us came close to overturning. I don't think it lasted over three minutes, but it seemed like a week."

The skipper and his son popped to the surface, gulping air in the narrow space between the water and the pilothouse's floor, now its ceiling. For a moment they were disoriented, looking at the floating objects around them.

"I broke the glass out of a window with my fist and cut my hand," said Gale. "The window was about twenty-five inches wide. I told Frankie to go out and swim to the land seventy-five yards away, He cut his back and legs on jagged glass. Frankie grabbed a piece of floating line and swam over and grabbed the keel. I found another window, busted that one out and swam out." Both men held on to the boat's keel, and the salt water made their wounds from broken glass burn like fire.

On a nearby shrimp boat, Teddy Atkinson said, "Oh, my God, Mr. Clyde—Captain Greek and Frankie are gone. All I see is the keel of their boat."

But in a moment, Atkinson and Captain Clyde Gault spotted Greek and Frankie, the tops of their heads barely showing above the keel. Gault and Atkinson pulled up their anchor, rescued the two men and offered them dry clothing, while another fisherman dove into the sea and cut the *Ella D*'s anchor rope.

The boat was towed out of the channel and dragged into shallow water. In those days, few shrimp boats had radios, and the U.S. Coast Guard had not yet learned of the accident.

Gale and his son were taken to a hospital for treatment of their wounds, and four days passed before they could pull the boat back to the docks and place it on the railway for repairs. It was not until then that Gale entered the pilothouse, surveyed the great damage and was surprised to observe that the little painting of Jesus walking on the water was still tacked to the wall.

Gale, a native of Camden County, said his father was in the timber business before becoming a commercial fisherman on the Altamaha River. His parents recently celebrated their sixty-seventh wedding anniversary.

Before buying a shrimp boat in 1948 for just $3,800—some of the big boats cost about $1,000 a foot today—Gale worked on Blackbeard Island for the federal government, did some house painting and served as a Darien policeman for ten years.

He hasn't been able to fish for several months because of occasional dizzy spells and headaches resulting from an injury in an accident that occurred as he installed doors on a shrimp net on his boat at the docks. A stretched nylon rope broke, hurling like a slingshot a piece of three-quarter-inch pipe into his face and smashing bone below and above his left eye. "It knocked me out for a few minutes," Gale said. "There were three stitches below my eye and four above it."

On a foggy autumn morning, Gale walked on the Darien docks, looking at several fishing boats and waving to a passing boat's skipper. He obviously was homesick for the sea.

"I hope to get back out there before much longer," he said.

Golden Dreams

AURARIA—A prospector told his wife at breakfast one day in the late 1920s that he had dreamed about a gold vein that ran little more than hollering distance from their house. Soon after Bill Trammell left for the gold-rich hills, Amy jotted down notes about his latest dream on the back of a calendar, thinking she could tease him later. But, as usual, the dreamer had the last laugh.

Less than two hours later, Trammell ran down a hill toward his house in Auraria, yelling, "Amy" nearly every breath and carrying forty-two dollars' worth of gold in his pan. Discovery of the precious metal surprised her because he had dug without success for two weeks in the same area.

"Bill said he had gone under the topsoil only a foot or two, but he never would have found the gold unless he had dreamed where it was," she said. "He dreamed he went over the hill, and below the cemetery he turned to the left and went down the hill until he found where an old chestnut tree fell and partly burned."

She added, "He stepped over the tree and there was a rock a layin' there. In the dream, he found the gold two feet from the rock."

Several days later, after digging thirty feet and following the gold vein, the couple realized they had crossed a man's land, so they stopped work and notified him. The landowner immediately sent a crew of men to the area to dig for gold in what became known as the Trammell Shoot.

Bill Trammell, "a gold miner from the cradle to the grave," was thirty-one years old when he and his seventeen-year-old bride settled down in Auraria

Amy Trammell searched for gold with her husband, Bill, for thirty-five years in red clay hills near Auraria in North Georgia. Two days before his death, he begged her to promise not to go underground again trying to find gold.

not far from the Lumpkin County area where Benjamin Parks discovered gold in 1828 in Cherokee Indian territory.

For thirty-five years they searched for gold, digging in the red clay hills and setting up sluice boxes in the streams. She learned to swing a mattock or push a shovel as well as any prospector, working winter days when the weather was so cold that she occasionally stood on a plank to keep her feet from freezing.

Their three sons reside in other states, and Bill has been dead about ten years, but Amy hasn't hung up her prospecting tools. "I'm not quit yet," she said. "Anytime I get the chance, I go back. I'm not gonna quit until I'm under the ground to stay."

Two days before his death, Bill begged Amy to promise that she would never go underground in search of gold again. Perhaps he had dreamed of tragedy, but he warned his wife she would be killed if she dug beneath the earth again.

Mrs. Trammell was almost trapped underground several times, but she never revealed the close calls to her family. "Bill could foresee things that were going to happen," she said. "It makes me shiver thinking about it. One day he called me out of a tunnel and said he had a feeling the ground was going to slide."

Speculating that old-time miners had dug another tunnel and weakened the earth, he told his wife, "You gonna keep on, and you're gonna get killed."

She laughed and replied, "It's a good way to be buried. You won't have to pay for it."

After he walked to the other side of the hill to look for another tunnel, she began digging on the surface. "I dug a foot or two, and I fell into the tunnel where I'd been working," said Mrs. Trammell. "It kept caving in, and I was two hours getting out of there."

Trammell returned to the area and said, "Amy, where in the world have you been?"

She said, "Just lookin' around."

Trammell revealed to his wife years later that he had a premonition about then-president John F. Kennedy's death, fearing the young chief executive would die in a city other than Washington before the end of his term.

Mrs. Trammell agreed she and her husband had to have faith to keep digging in the hills year after year in search of gold. "The gold in the earth is just like love and faith," she said. "You can just feel that it's there somewhere, but you can't see it. You've got to work hard to get it."

She strongly believes that a large amount of "the purest gold in the world" still lies waiting to be discovered in these hills around Auraria. "Gold will do something to you," said Mrs. Trammell. "It will make you go out in the cold, make you get up early whether you want to or not and get back to it. And you will go through anything. You'll go hungry to go out and stay in that hole to dig."

Sometimes on walks in the woods near Auraria, she thinks about the nineteenth-century prospectors and their dreams of great wealth. "You can go out on any hill and down in any valley around Auraria, and you'll see the old-timers' works, the holes they dug, the ditches they cut, the gravel piles they left," she said. "It makes you stand and wonder who did this, and did they make anything? You know they had to be gettin' some, or they wouldn't have kept digging and doing all that hard work."

Short, Sweet and Cheap Weddings

WARES CROSSROADS—Most of the hundreds of marriage ceremonies conducted by William "Pete" Ware in twelve years as justice of the peace were short, sweet and cheap.

"I've married 'em every hour," said Ware at his Wares Crossroads home in Troup County. "I 'spect I married 40 percent of 'em between twelve midnight and daylight."

Some of the couples were even married on credit, and he didn't collect a nickel from a few. Frankly, I can't quite imagine a starry-eyed couple saying, "I do," and then requesting, "Charge it, please."

Ware, who is in his late forties, drives a county school bus and has a business shop on U.S. 27, just north of LaGrange. Under this single roof, a person can ask for radio and television repairs, get a haircut, take guitar lessons or seek services of the notary public.

Ware no longer serves as a justice of the peace. The law in this county was changed so that duties of the JPs are now handled by a small claims court. He ran for the position of judge but lost in a runoff to Mrs. Ellen Hobby.

An old sign listing marriage prices still hangs next to a mule collar and the front door of Pete Ware's shop. The weddings that he conducted, though quite informal and devoid of music unless the couple asked him to play "Here Comes the Bride" on his guitar, were bargains. The price list includes:

Regular weddings...$5.
Long weddings...$10.
Short weddings...$4.
Short short weddings...$3.
Shotgun weddings (with gun)...$6.
Shotgun weddings (gun furnished)...$7.
Midnight weddings...$12.
Special: One haircut, one guitar lesson, one wedding, one telephone call,
   all for $11.

He only remembers one man and woman who requested the "special." He also recalls that one man married the same woman three times. The oldest person he married was an eighty-four-year-old man who wed a woman only twenty-eight years old. The woman refused to step out of the car for the ceremony. Many of the brides were young and pregnant.

He could legally marry a pregnant girl under eighteen years of age to the father-to-be if she obtained a physician's signed statement that she was expecting a baby and they also got a marriage license from a probate judge and met other qualifications there.

Former justice of the peace Pete Ware conducted marriage ceremonies at bargain prices, and some couples were even wed on credit. He estimated about 40 percent of the weddings took place between midnight and sunrise.

In several instances, the expectant brides were from wealthy families in this section, and marriages were arranged for midnight or later so they would draw little or no local attention.

Were there many shotgun weddings? "Yes, a lot of 'em, but not with shotguns," said Ware. "They got too lazy to tote a shotgun. I remember one father who had a gun in his belt when he came with his daughter and the boy."

In another affair, an angry father was hot on the trail of his daughter and her fiancé but arrived too late for the ceremony. "A car with a boy and a girl in it whooped in here," said Ware. "I knew the boy. He said he wanted to get married right quick. I noticed he kept lookin' up the road. I married 'em. He said, 'I'll pick up the certificate when I come back by.'"

The newlyweds rushed to the car, but the motor wouldn't start, and the groom jerked up the hood and fixed it. Then they dashed away and in seconds had topped the hill and were out of sight.

"Then another car whooped in here, and it was her daddy and somebody else," said Ware. "He said, 'Which way did they go?' And, I said, 'That way, but they're married.'"

The bride's father replied, "I'm gonna kill 'im if I catch 'im."

Fortunately, the girl's father cooled off and never harmed the groom, said Ware, who pointed out that the couple has two children and appears to be happy.

In another marriage ceremony, a bride weighing about three hundred pounds fainted, knocking down a heater and three chairs. "We washed her face and got her up," said Ware. "This little bitty man had come in with her. I don't know if she was drunk. It was hot in that room. We picked her up and toted her to the car, and she mumbled, 'Get my pocketbook.' I said, 'Get up. You are just excited about the wedding.' She said, 'No, I've been married three times.'"

A highlight of his career was a bit part as a taxi driver in the movie *Deliverance*, filmed in Georgia and starring Burt Reynolds. "It was something different to do," he said. "I didn't care that much about it. It's more like being around a carnival."

PART II

Life's Work

Fightin' Mad

RUCKERSVILLE—Windell Cleveland never has read *Gone With the Wind*, but he and Tara owner Gerald O'Hara share the same feeling—a great love for the land. Cleveland, thirty-six, has heard his father, Cade, seventy-nine, say the same things about Georgia soil that O'Hara told his daughter, Scarlett. Land is something very precious that the Lord has provided for man to use with care; no more is being made on this earth, and you should never let go of the soil you own, the old man in Elbert County believes.

Windell and Cade Cleveland fervently hope and pray that they will live the rest of their days on the farm that has been in their family more than 150 years.

In recent months, they have attended public meetings, written letters to President Carter and members of Congress and contacted many Georgians to express strong opposition to the Richard B. Russell Dam and lake that would swallow the Cleveland farm. They were overjoyed to learn that Carter will not seek funds in his 1978 budget for the Russell Dam. And the Clevelands believe there's a good chance Congress will support Carter.

Windell Cleveland knelt and picked up a handful of soil in a freshly planted corn field on his farm about four hundred yards from the Savannah River and twelve miles east of Elberton. "This bottom land in here—I don't care where you go," he said, letting the soil sprinkle between his fingers, "you won't find richer land in the state of Georgia or nowhere else. This is some of the richest in the world. Eight acres here I planted in corn. I wish you'd seen the corn that

The year "1741" was scratched on a brick in this chimney at the house where Windell Cleveland's father, Cade Cleveland, was born. Settlers apparently reached this area only eight years after General James Oglethorpe established the Georgia colony in Savannah.

come off this river bottom land last year." Each spring he plants a variety of vegetables on his 152-acre tract and five other farms that he rents.

Although President Carter has decided to scrap the Russell Dam because of environmental concerns, the uprooting of sixty families and other factors, the U.S. Army Corps of Engineers is continuing construction on the project and still acquiring tracts of land with its funds from 1977's budget.

The Clevelands—Windell; his wife, Charlene; daughter Audry, thirteen; and father, Cade—are determined to keep their farm. A corps official told Windell that much of the farm would be covered by the twenty-six-thousand-acre lake and the rest would be used for recreational areas.

Cade Cleveland keeps three loaded shotguns and a .32-caliber revolver "for them rogues, thieves and corps of engineers," and he vows that nobody is going to handcuff him in his house and force him off the farm. The old man strongly hopes that he won't ever have to fire a gun in anger, but if anyone attempts to drive him off the land, "I figure I'll take one or two with me."

Windell said that corps Project Manager Jim Ellis in Elberton advised him that if a landowner refused to leave after condemnation of a farm, federal marshals would be ordered to move the people away. "I looked him straight in the eye and said, 'You know that thing could work a heap of ways besides one...when you go to puttin' somebody out of his house,'" said Windell.

He, his wife and their daughter reside in mobile homes on a hill a short distance from his father's fifty-year-old house. On a tour of the farm, Windell pointed out the two-story wooden house in which his father was born. Scratched on a brick in one of the two chimneys is the year "1741,"

Windell Cleveland says the Savannah River bottomland on his farm near Elberton has some of the richest soil found in Georgia. He hopes and prays that he and his family will be allowed to live there the rest of their days.

suggesting that settlers traveled up the river eight years after General James Oglethorpe established the Georgia colony in Savannah.

The nearby Ruckersville community was settled by John Rucker and John White, who moved to Georgia in 1773 from Virginia.

Windell Cleveland feels that the loss of his farm to the corps of engineers would be as painful as death. "It's not takin' your life, but, in other words, it's the same as takin' your life…takin' something you worked for years to build up," he said. "Then some guys come along sayin' you got to move out. My daddy cleared this land with an ax long before the chainsaws came along."

He drove a Jeep past some twenty-two old houses, barns, sheds and outbuildings used to store farm equipment and hay and then showed me field after field that he plowed and planted this spring. "I worked hard on this place over the years, day and night," he said. "I love to see stuff grow. And I've got as pretty a bunch of goats as you ever saw. If they come and take what we've got and everything…I'm out."

Looking across a field where watermelons will grow this summer, he added, "I don't know of nothin' I could do. Farmin' is all I know. It's something I've done since I got out of high school in '59—and before then."

A supporter of the Russell Dam has said that the forest on both sides of the Savannah River is home to very little wildlife. Numerous times as we walked or rode slowly across the farm and over the river bottomlands, Windell stopped and pointed out tracks of wild turkeys and deer. He could hardly believe his ears when a proponent of the dam said at a public hearing that a deer swimming in this part of the Savannah River would have to pack his lunch.

"People don't realize what's out on this river," said Windell. "They don't know what the dam and lake's gonna destroy. There's lots of wildlife—deer, turkeys, 'coons, possum, squirrels, bobcats, fox. I believe there's over $800,000 worth of timber, if the dam is built, that they'll lose in South Carolina. There's some of the finest timber up and down the river. It grows fast, and it grows big and tall."

Windell's father said, "And there'll never be anymore of that if this dam is built."

The old man said the lake would back right up to his little fish pond, where he catches catfish every spring and summer. "I wouldn't take $10,000 for my fishpond if somebody laid it down in my hand," he declared.

Windell believes supporters of the dam have a weak argument in saying the reservoir would provide a large amount of hydroelectric power sorely needed in this area. "The Hartwell dam up here…," he said, "they don't run it [release water to generate power] but four to six hours a day. Back yonder when we was havin' cold weather, they was hollerin' shortage of power. I watched that river. They run it an average of six hours. In the summertime, they don't run it but two and a half hours. Since the meeting [a recent public hearing in Anderson, South Carolina] when I got up and told 'em the way they operated it, you know, them jokers have been turnin' water through on Saturday and Sunday for two weekends. That's how 'low-down' they are."

In addition to the twenty-eight thousand acres that the reservoir would cover, the corps is trying to buy another thirty-three thousand acres of land that would be used for access roads, boat launching areas, parking lots and recreational areas. "Land is precious," said Windell. "I tell you, people don't realize what it means. That's a heap of land out of use. No more good. They know them kind of power plants don't make much power. If they want power, why don't they build a steam plant with a small lake? I tell you, the corps of engineers wants a big job, and they done went too far. You puttin' one dam in use, and you're destroyin' wildlife, timber and our farmin'. We don't need that dam."

The corps estimated the dam and lake would cost $248 million plus another $75 million for pumped storage facilities. So far it has spent nearly $31 million on the project. President Carter decided against requesting $21 million for the Russell Dam in his 1978 budget.

Windell and Cade Cleveland hope Congress never provides another dime for the dam. And they'd like to see the corps tear down what crews already have built at the dam site.

POSTSCRIPT: The U.S. Army Corps of Engineers eventually built the dam and in 1984 flooded nearly 27,000 acres of land to create Lake Russell. After insisting for years that it needed all of the Clevelands' land, the corps compromised. It bought 126 acres, leaving Windell and his family 36 acres. It's enough to live on but, as Windell points out today, not enough to farm. He and his wife Charlene have a breathtaking view of the lake, but they don't fish and rarely take the short walk from their house to the water's edge.

Hear the full update on the Clevelands by Chuck Salter at www. thisamericanlife.org, episode 413, "Georgia Rambler."

J.B., Thunder and the Lord in Fields

PORTERDALE—J.B. Loyd had just finished eating lunch after spending the morning hoeing the weeds from rows of vegetables growing in a field beside his Newton County farm home. His weather-beaten straw hat lay nearby as Loyd, wearing overalls, propped his bare feet on the arm of a sofa.

"I got an old horse out yonder named Thunder," said Loyd, sixty-five, whose farm is four miles from Porterdale. "He's got the day off today. I plow him a lot of days nearly twelve hours. One day I came in from the field, and sweat was all over Thunder. My wife said, 'J.B., you've been workin' Thunder too hard. Look how he's sweatin'.' I said, 'What do you think about ol' J.B.?' I was as hot as Thunder."

Observing that the hotter a horse gets the faster he walks pulling a plow, Loyd said he recently underwent a physical examination and asked a nurse to be sure to record his height.

"And she said, 'J.B., you haven't grown any.'" Loyd said, "I told her I went out there yesterday morning plowin' that horse, and that horse got to walkin' fast. I said my overall was draggin' the ground when I started, and at dinnertime, it was up to my knees. Don't tell me I haven't grown. I was a foot taller than when I went out to the field."

The sight of a man plowing with a horse in 1976 makes some passing motorists do a double-take. He always waves at the cars, whether he knows the occupants or not.

"If there's anything that makes me mad…You'll be plowing right beside the road, and somebody will come by," said Loyd. "You throw up your hand

and they don't wave back at you. That makes you feel bad. People in the country—they wave back at you. One day I waved and a fellow said, 'Who's that?' I said I didn't know, and he asked why I waved."

The farmer explained, "I said I wave at everybody who goes up and down this road. If I see 'em, I wave. I love to live and have friends, where, when I need a favor, I don't have to back up to get it. Face a man and get it."

While working in the fields, Loyd knows some of his happiest hours, and though weary and wet with sweat, he is at peace with the world. "I told a man the other day, when I got out in the field, there wasn't nobody out there but me, ol' Thunder and the good Lord. It's a lot of hard work, but you get somethin' out there you don't get nowhere else. You think about everything that happened a long, long time ago while plowin'."

If his death doesn't come in a hospital or in his home, Loyd would like to die in his fields. "I told some of 'em I hoped I died out there because it seems like I'm nearer the good Lord in the field than anywhere else, workin' the soil."

Loyd acknowledged that it requires a lot of faith to be a farmer and much more is necessary than merely throwing out the seeds and asking the Lord to make a good crop. "Now, mister, you've got to do your part," said Loyd. "He's gonna do his. You go out there and plant and trust him. I never plant a row of nothin' that I don't ask the Lord to add his blessing to it when I stop."

Loyd spent about twenty years working at the lunch counter in a Porterdale store owned by the late Jack Elliott, father of *Outdoor Life* magazine writer Charlie Elliott of Covington. He remembers days in the early 1930s when hot dogs, hamburgers and soft drinks were bought for a nickel each by the local millworkers, some of whom purchased a week's supply of groceries for three to five dollars.

Loyd said the elder Elliott was not only his boss but also his frequent hunting companion and a true friend who helped him when he was in need. Jack Elliott lent him the money to buy his farm and also aided him once when Mrs. Loyd was hospitalized.

He also vividly remembers during Christmas week in the mid-1930s when he made his weekly ten-dollar payment on the home loan and then received a receipt and the ten dollars back with this suggestion: "Go buy your wife a Christmas present with this." He did.

Loyd believes that young people today "have a hard row to hoe" and face numerous temptations while lacking an appreciation for the value of a dollar. "When I was growin' up, I used to plow for a fellow from sunup to sundown," he said. "He'd pay off every night, and I'll tell you what he paid me—fifty cents. He gave it to me in pennies. Yes, fifty pennies every night after twelve hours behind a mule. That was in the 1930s."

Farmer J.B. Loyd says that when he is plowing, there's nobody in the field except him, his horse Thunder and the good Lord. He believes there are three things that money cannot buy—love, happiness and friendship.

Loyd said he has learned there are three things that money cannot buy—love, happiness and friendship. He believes peace of mind is very important for an abundant life. "I try to live so that when I go to bed at night, I've got nothing but a clear conscience."

The farmer said that if people obey their parents, they "won't have any trouble with the rest" of the Ten Commandments. "I loved my mother and daddy," Loyd said. "My daddy was ninety-one years old the day he died, and I still said, 'Yes, sir' and 'No, sir.' You don't hear that much anymore."

He has fond memories of Christmastime more than fifty years ago, when a "nickel stick of peppermint candy" was the most prized gift under the tree. "My brother and I would get up in the night to see if Santa Claus had come yet, and we'd take candy and nuts to the bed," he said. "If mother heard us, she got on us about it."

One year his mother told him that if he and his brother picked a lot of cotton, Santa Claus might be able to bring them a bicycle. Needless to say, the boys met the goal, and Santa delivered as promised.

As a youngster, Loyd could pick 100 to 150 pounds of cotton a day, but as an adult trying to pay for his wife's surgery, he walked two miles to a farm and picked 300 pounds a day.

Adventure on Satilla River

WAYCROSS—A four-day float trip on a huge timber raft to a sawmill on the Satilla River was a memorable adventure for a young fellow, says a Ware County farmer. Fred Voigt, seventy-eight, who has grown pecans and tobacco for more than half a century down here in wiregrass country, was living with his parents on their Pierce County farm when he got his first timber-selling assignment.

When the Voigts moved from Atlanta to the Forks of the River community six miles from Blackshear in 1914, the unexploited forests had beautiful, virgin timber. Some of the yellow pines were twenty-four to thirty inches in diameter, and the lowest limbs were fifty to sixty feet above the sandy soil.

Voigt said that every year or two there was a freshet—a sudden overflowing from heavy rains—on the Satilla River. "The woods were flooded, and this was the occasion to have cash from timber," he said. "We went into the swamps a mile or two from the river and cut logs, winter or summer, standing waist deep in water, with a cross-cut saw."

Usually half a dozen families joined hands in the effort, each making a raft from forty to fifty giant logs. Long iron pins with rings on top were driven into the middle of each log, and heavy Manila rope was threaded through the loops. The first sawmill was located downstream at Atkinson in Brantley County, and the second was at Burnt Fort.

"My first experience in this was in August," said Voigt. "We had six rafts of timber, and a boy or two from each family went with each raft. We took the highest floating logs and made a kitchen raft and nailed boards on the logs

Fred Voigt, who grew up on a southeast Georgia farm, and several friends assembled six huge rafts of timber and traveled four days down the Satilla River to a sawmill in an adventure that he fondly remembers.

and put wagon loads of dirt on there. You couldn't turn the rafts loose on the Satilla until the water receded to within the bank, or the rafts could float out on a hill and leave you stranded."

Remembering how crooked the old Satilla was, I could appreciate the great caution needed to negotiate those many bends in a log raft. "You'd let the big raft drift in current to the end of a long cove, and it would strike the bank and swing back out," said Voigt. "The river is so crooked, it's a slow, painful process rounding those bends."

The young men had to maintain a considerable distance between rafts to avoid a major logjam if one became lodged in trees. "We'd turn one raft loose with a man on it, and when it was out of sight we would turn the next one loose," he said. "If something went wrong, a boy would holler. They loved to holler. It was similar to a yodel, and the sound carried way up the river."

At night, the young farmers tied up their rafts at the bank, gathered firewood, set out bush hooks and caught catfish for supper. "Remember this was in August," said Voigt. "We hadn't gone around more than one bend before a cool thunderstorm started. We jumped into the warm river rather than take that cold rain. So we stayed wet for three days and three nights. Each of us had brought only one change of clothes in a suitcase. We were so exhausted and wet and had been unable to sleep."

When the six log rafts finally reached the Atkinson sawmill and were secured in a chained-off area, an appraiser examined the timber and reported to the office. "One of us went to get the check," said Voigt, "and it was only ten o'clock in the morning, but we were so exhausted we lay down on the kitchen raft and fell asleep. You could have fired a shotgun over their heads and you wouldn't have awakened those boys."

They later boarded the train that went from Brunswick to Waycross and began a slow journey home. Voigt laughed and said, "The train stopped at every pig trail. Anybody could flag it down with a handkerchief."

They stepped off the train at the Schlatterville community, which everybody in South Georgia pronounces "slaughterville," and discovered the Satilla was out of its banks once again after thundershowers. "The river had flooded the woods and a dirt road for a mile," said Voigt. "We took off our clothes, tied them up and held them over our heads and waded. Each of us held several burning light'ard splinters up as torches to see that night. We walked through the flooded flat woods and finally got to what we called 'the hill.'"

After drying themselves beside a campfire, the young men dressed and walked on the dirt road back to their farm homes.

While still a teenager, Voigt made trips every Thursday with his father in a wagon filled with vegetables, syrup, hay, pork and beef to Waycross for sale on the streets. "We had to leave home at 1:00 a.m. to get to Waycross by 6:00 a.m.," he said. "It was fourteen miles on a woods road by the river to an old wooden bridge and on to town. Many times in the winter, it was so cold Daddy and I had to stop on the road and build a fire with big, fat light'ard stumps to warm ourselves."

I guess Fred Voigt is amused when young people today complain about little inconveniences that they take so seriously. Folks in his generation accepted hardships as a natural part of their way of life.

Last of the Polite Tobacco Chewers

GLADES—Country store owner Hugh Wiley's antique tobacco cutter, like an old gray mule, "ain't what she used to be." If one section were welded, the cast-iron gadget could be in shape once again to cut the mustard—or, rather, the tobacco.

But times have changed, and things like tobacco cutters and mules are merely objects of curiosity nowadays. Most kids in cities today probably couldn't identify either one.

Wiley, who bought this store on Georgia 52 in Hall County fifteen miles north of Gainesville in 1954, sells bags of loose-leaf tobacco and the pre-cut, packaged plugs. However, the late J.D. Rogers, who built the store in 1903, probably cut miles of tobacco plugs with the device.

Wiley, sixty-two, who enjoys chewing tobacco every day, said, "It's still going fairly strong. Loose-leaf tobacco sells best. The ones chewing are mostly middle-aged and older. Not too many of the younger boys want to chew," he said. "They're missing a good thing."

My only experience in chewing tobacco was a nauseating failure. During recess in the ninth grade in Waycross, I accidentally swallowed some juice, and minutes later I turned rather green in a biology class.

Wiley gave me a sympathetic look and explained that chewing tobacco can be a pleasant and relaxing pastime. "Swallowing the juice won't turn you against it," he said. "You can get sick on bananas or candy, and you won't want any for a while. It won't completely turn you against tobacco."

The merchant suggested that the habit might be good for digestion. Apparently there is a lot more to chewing tobacco than I suspected.

Hugh Wiley displays the antique tobacco cutter in his country store at Glades, Georgia. He enjoys chewing tobacco every day and suggests it might be good for digestion, but he finds few youths are taking up the habit.

"You've got different types of chewing," Wiley said. "Some people chew it—I mean they're cutting it—and spit a lot. I don't chew like that. I can use one chew of tobacco for hours. I just let it lie there in my cheek and maybe move it sometimes."

It never dawned on me that some folks are strictly one-sided chewers. Wiley, who impressed me as being a good conservative, leans to the left when he's chewing. "I always chew on my left side," he said, chuckling. "It's just where you start, I suppose. You couldn't put my hat on where it'd suit me, either. I'd want to move it."

Another reason that I didn't become a tobacco chewer was that I never learned how to spit with the style and class that my Waycross friends developed. Stained toes on my shoes would have marked me strictly as an amateur. "Yes, there's an art to spitting," said Wiley, who must be among the last of the polite tobacco chewers. He doesn't chew in his country store or in his home. "I broke myself from chewing in the store on account of the different types of spitters. Had a lot of buddies come in who couldn't spit accurately or far enough and missed the spittoons. They got tobacco juice on the floor, so I moved the spittoons out."

In his youth, did the girls object to their dates enjoying a "chaw of tobacco"? Wiley laughed and said, "I think the guys would leave their tobacco out while they were courting."

A Garden Dedicated to God

GAINESVILLE—A very close brush with death in a car/train wreck eleven years ago deepened Ted Higgins's faith in God and led to a passionate interest in horticulture. His friends in North Georgia are awed by the retired homebuilder and cabinetmaker's genius in growing flowers, fruits and vegetables of great beauty and extraordinary size.

"My garden is dedicated to God," said Ted, sixty-nine, as he showed me plants with ancestors from foreign nations. Among them were tomatoes from China and Western Europe, pear trees from Egypt, peanuts from Kenya and fig trees from Turkey. His most unusual American vegetable was giant cabbages from Alaska.

His survival in the smashup near Buford was miraculous. Higgins's car's brakes failed. A freight train hit the auto and then pushed the tangled wreckage 102 feet down the tracks. "Rolling down the tracks, I saw the engineer twice before I came out of the seat," he said. "A deputy sheriff saw it happen, and at first he couldn't get me out of the car. I was drowning in gasoline. The right side of the car was hit. The car was turned over by a wrecker to get me out. When I cut the switch off, I said, 'Here it is. It's yours, God.'"

His arms were torn from their sockets, his head was cut severely by pieces of glass, his spinal cord was damaged and his body was blistered by gasoline. "It took 385 stitches in my head, and the back of my head has been cut open thirty times in eleven years to remove glass that gets on nerves," he said. "In the hospital, my left arm couldn't pick up a magazine. Now I can pick up thirty pounds with my left hand and fifty pounds with my right hand. I had

Life's Work

Ted Higgins of Gainesville grows some of the biggest tomatoes in Georgia, and some of his fruits and vegetables have ancestors in other countries. He studied horticulture while recovering from injuries in a car/train wreck.

no feelings in these fingers or the inside of my legs. I can drop a piece of hot steel and I don't know it's there until I smell it burning."

During four long years of recuperation from multiple injuries, Ted read everything about horticulture that he could get his hands on. "To keep from going crazy, I started studying soils, soil analysis, propagation of plants, fertilizers, how to make virgin soil, organic chemistry."

He learned that a Hall County woman, a European native married to a former soldier, was growing big tomatoes from seeds she'd brought from her homeland. The plants were eight feet tall before developing limbs, and they reached to the top of a wooden porch, where tomatoes lay ripening on the roof.

The woman gave Higgins twelve tomatoes that weighed a total of twenty-six pounds, and with these seeds, he began selective propagation to improve an already superior species. "The biggest tomato I have grown yet weighed 4⅛ pounds and lacked a quarter inch of covering a ten-inch dinner plate," he said. "I had the world record until year before last. A fellow grew a 6½ pounder. I bought some seeds but couldn't grow them as big."

One summer he picked fifty tomatoes that weighed from 3 to 3⅛ pounds each. "I took them to the curb market, and I could not sell them," he said. "They wouldn't pay $1.50 for a tomato. But they would pay $0.50 a pound for my little tomatoes." However, a friend from North Carolina bought every one of the giant tomatoes and then returned to buy another $100 worth.

Ted has grown radishes weighing up to eighteen pounds each. With the aid of forty-watt light bulbs to extend the growing hours, he has grown Alaskan cabbage weighing thirty pounds. "I learned they had twenty-one hours of daylight in Alaska in June," Ted said. "So I didn't let my plants go to sleep here. They grew for twenty-four hours a day."

His Spanish peanuts from Kenya grew to astounding sizes, and he picked a bushel every twenty-six vines. A realtor paid him five dollars each for five shells—the longest was five inches and the others were four inches each and were filled with the giant nuts.

Ted also has grown very big lettuce, and he has developed a variety of collard that won't give off an offensive odor while cooking.

If Ted had been a fisheries biologist, I imagine he would have figured out a way to grow eight-pound bluegills and twenty-five-pound largemouth bass.

Ted was kind enough to share with me some of his secrets for growing tomatoes. In February, he plants in his greenhouse seeds whose ancestors grew in soil of Western Europe. By mid-April, he has plants eight to ten inches tall for his own use and for sale to fellow tomato lovers. He digs a hole twenty-four inches in diameter and eighteen inches deep for each of his plants.

"I mix three tablespoons of Epsom salts, three cups of 5-10-10 fertilizer, five cups of mason lime and a peck of cow manure and stir it in that hole of rich dirt," he said. "I wet it down for a week or ten days before setting out the tomato plants. The reason you must wait is that the lime and fertilizer will gas your tomato plants while dissipating."

He added, "After 10 days, it's all bled into the soil. Then you can grow tomatoes. These extra large tomatoes take around 140 days to develop. That's about three weeks longer than other tomatoes."

Each month, he serves his tomato plants two tablespoons of Epsom salts in water and one spoon of Borax in a gallon of water. The Epsom salts help break down the fertilizer and make it easier for the plant to digest. The Borax is needed because of its deficiency in North Georgia soil.

"Each week I put one tablespoon of Miracle-Gro liquid fertilizer in a gallon of water," he said. "Keep the top on the plastic jug. Make several small holes in the bottom so the liquid can seep through into the soil."

Ted reminded me that if I saw a plant develop bloom rot, this meant that the soil was lacking in lime. Rather than use agricultural lime, which takes five years to dissipate, he favors an application of mason lime each year.

Some of his tomatoes grow so large that he averages picking one hundred pounds from each of the plants. A slice of tomato extends over the edges of a slice of white bread. He uses a wire loop around each plant so that the limbs won't snap.

"Alternate the areas where you grow tomatoes or the nematodes will get them," Ted said. "Or you could dig the hole, remove the dirt and replace it with new dirt, and you could plant there year after year."

Last summer he was successful with a couple of weird experiments—growing tomatoes on a battery charger and roses on an electrostatic fence. I wonder how on Earth that was done.

Legend about Good Luck

SUGAR VALLEY—I've heard all of my life that a horseshoe will bring a person good luck. Some folks even nail a horseshoe, open end at the top, over a door, believing it will prevent their good luck from spilling out. Not until I met blacksmith Judd Nelson, sixty-six, of Sugar Valley in Gordon County did I learn how it got started.

Nelson was told the horseshoe legend a few months ago when he demonstrated his work at Greenville, South Carolina. "A fellow asked me if I knew the legend about good luck, and I said I didn't," said Nelson. "He said it goes that the devil needed shoes to be put on, and he'd go to a blacksmith. The shoes would be put on, and the devil would run off without paying.

"He'd go to another blacksmith and have him put 'em on and leave and not pay him. Next one he went to, the blacksmith got the shoes ready and told the helper, 'Just put 'em on him while they're hot.' And he put 'em on and the devil left a' runnin' and never did go back to any of the blacksmiths."

Children watching Nelson work at the Prater's Mill Country Fair each spring and fall near Dalton sometimes ask him why horses need shoes. "I told 'em shoes keep a horse from wearin' his feet out, makes 'em travel better," said Nelson. "At the blacksmiths' convention one year, some New York girls wondered why we put shoes on mules.

"My friend Carl Dance from Rome said, 'This country is so rough I have to shoe huntin' dogs down here [in Georgia].' And I said, 'Yeah, I've seen dogs' shoes wear out, and they'd run their legs off.'"

Judd Nelson of Sugar Valley, near Calhoun, has operated a blacksmith's shop since 1935, when he nailed four shoes onto a horse's feet for only $1.10. Once, Nelson put new shoes on a horse in a total of only thirty minutes.

Nelson has been operating a blacksmith's shop in Sugar Valley, six miles northwest of Calhoun, since 1935, when he was providing four horseshoes and nailing them on a horse's feet for $1.10. He recently paid $1.10 for each of four horseshoes that he planned to use for some "fancy, ornamental" wrought-iron objects.

"I have put on four horseshoes in thirty minutes, and I have put on four in half a day," he said, grinning. "There was one mule that we had to throw down and tie his feet together before I could put the shoes on." His own record was set one day in the midst of the Depression when he nailed twenty-four shoes on horses' feet in only two hours and forty-five minutes. Another day, Nelson and a helper put on eighty-two horseshoes.

"There are thirty-two nails to a set of horseshoes, eight nails to the shoe," he said. "A lot of folks used to come up and say, 'Would you shoe my horse and let me pay a penny for the first nail and double for all the rest of 'em?' That's two pennies for the second, four cents for the third, eight cents for the fourth and so on. I said I'd do it for that."

Nelson laughed and said his wife sometimes says he's the only man she ever met who could put both of his feet in his mouth at the same time. "I told her I always kicked 'em out one way or the other," he said, chuckling.

Has he ever met a female blacksmith? "I met one named Dorothy at the blacksmiths' convention in Illinois," Nelson said. "She was thirty-one and from Washington and had some pretty fancy forging. I admired her work. Fact of the business, I said, 'You are the prettiest blacksmith I've ever seen. You are the only one I ever seen I wouldn't mind kissin' goodbye.'

"And, she said, 'Judd, what're you waitin' for?' I told my wife when I got home I did something I never did before. She said, 'What?' I said I'd kissed a blacksmith goodbye. She looked kinda funny." Then he tried again to get both of his feet out of his mouth.

"I just work when I take a notion," said Nelson, watching pieces of iron grow hot on his forge in the barn next to his nineteenth-century farmhouse. "I sit down when I take a notion. Somebody comes along, and I'll sit down and talk." A watch rests in a pocket of his overalls, but he isn't concerned with any kind of schedule.

I observed that a hardworking blacksmith must work up a big appetite. "He'll eat all right," said Nelson, reaching for the hammer to forge a piece of wrought iron on the two-hundred-pound anvil that his father, Bill Nelson, bought in 1918. "Doesn't matter what's in the bowl just as long as it's a big one most of the time. A blacksmith can sleep pretty well, too."

Has he had much trouble with stubborn mules? "You can knock a mule to make him go, but a horse is different," said Nelson. "He won't take any knockin'. Trouble I've found is the owner. That mule will find out whether you're boss and take advantage of you. I never did pay much attention to the mule. It was the man that owned it. Do what he ought to, and the mule was all right."

Shaving Horse Gives Close Shave

TURNERS CORNER—The bearded old mountain man, who has more energy than many men half his age, dragged a wooden contraption out of his workshop. Oscar Cannon had a mischievous twinkle in his eyes and a big grin on his face when he looked at the visitor from Atlanta and asked, "You know what this thing is?"

It was immediately obvious to him that this native of the city of Ocilla was sho' nuff stumped by the strange-looking thing. "This is a shaving horse," said Cannon, eighty-one.

I almost blurted out, "Like the ones used in the old days, when a shave and a haircut cost just two bits?"

But silence is not only golden; it also suggests that a fellow is smart enough to wait for an explanation. I did.

"They used a shaving horse to make plow handles, ax handles and other handles for farm tools," said Cannon. "You used a drawing knife, like this one, to shave off strips of wood." The drawing knife didn't draw any pictures, but a fellow could grip the handles on both ends and do an awful lot of shaving on a piece of wood.

The shaving horse had a long front leg and two shorter back legs. Cannon showed me how he sits on the back of the "horse" and then puts his feet on the two pedals to lock a piece of wood in a vise-like grip in order to shave it into proper shape.

"You can shave the wood faster than you could in a vise," he explained. "They used this to shave poles and make barrels, too. I made this shaving

Oscar Cannon of Turners Corner said this old shaving horse was used to make handles for axes, plows and other farm tools. He made this one after finding a white oak that may have been one hundred years old.

horse. That white oak might have been one hundred years old. One day I was in the woods and saw this crooked tree and said to myself, 'That'll make a good shaving horse.'" So he cut down the tree, sawed the trunk into blocks and rolled them down the hill.

On a rainy day in the forest, while he was checking on the spring that supplies water for his home, Cannon stopped and stared with interest at a big bush. "This feller said, 'What'cha lookin' at?' And I told him, 'There's a set of plow handles in that bush.' And I saw a tree and told him, 'There are two sets in that one.'"

What kind of jobs did he do in his long years of work?

"Well, I guess if you refine it right down to the right principle, it'd be nothing,'" said Cannon, smiling.

Actually, the tall, slender man farmed for many years, did a considerable amount of carpentry and, in the late 1920s, helped build some mountain roads for the grand pay of fifteen cents an hour. For several years in the 1930s, he drove a truck, converted into a bus, and hauled kids to school for just fifty dollars a month.

Mr. and Mrs. Cannon have electricity and some other modern conveniences in their mountain home, but they don't feel the need for a telephone. Neither do they have a television set. They tried a TV set for two weeks and decided the noise and awful programs weren't desirable in their quiet home. At night, Cannon tries to find a worthwhile song on his radio, but sometimes it takes nearly three hours of station-switching before he hears a good one.

Each day he awakens with a desire to do an honest day's work.

He would offer this advice to young people: "Be honest and straight and work hard, and you'll have a chance to do all right. You can lie down and sleep at night and have no worries about who might wake you up at the wrong time."

Pointing to a painting of Jesus on his living room wall, Cannon said, "I get my guidance from Jesus Christ and the Bible."

The mountain man said he loves and also fears the Lord, and he tries to live as the Bible recommends. "He's the one I'm afraid of," Cannon said. "Lots of folks say they're afraid of the devil. But the Lord knows what we're doin' all the time, and you can't hide from him. He knows what you're thinkin' about and what you plan to do."

What kind of diet has enabled him to live nearly eighty-two years? "I've never eaten much meat," he said. "I eat lots of vegetables. My wife says, 'You need to eat more meat.' And I tell her, 'How 'bout them Chinamen over there who eat nothin' but rice? They live to be pretty old. Nothin' wrong with them.'"

In 1940, a doctor told Cannon he had a kidney disease and perhaps would live no more than four months. "I was depressed," Cannon said. "Had a big family, kids at home. I started praying to live, to get better, and that wouldn't work. So I turned the other way and asked God to help me get ready and willing to die. Everything eased off, and I felt like I was floatin' down the Mississippi River that evening. And I've been depending on my special doctor, Jesus Christ, ever since. There's no better one."

Cannon, who raised six daughters and three sons, chuckled and said, "I'm too independent and too stout to get on welfare."

Message of Hope, Faith and Love

MADISON—Lucy Mae Armour sat with hands clasped in her lap in a cane-bottom chair on the weather-beaten porch of a little, dilapidated, frame house at Madison. She wore a simple cotton dress, sneakers, a fishing cap with a bill and dark glasses that shielded her aging eyes from the bright morning sunshine.

Mrs. Armour, sixty-four, observing she has loved spirituals since first hearing them from the lips of her mother on a farm over in Putnam County, said, "When you sing a spiritual, it's from the heart and mind. It moves you all over. You can't be still. Anything without God in it...it doesn't last long. You put God in whatever you do, you'll come out all right."

Then her voice filled the air in song, as the message of hope, faith and love in the spiritual bridged the present and the past, reminding one of weary workers trudging back home from the cotton fields at the end of the day.

"Oh, be ready when he comes," Mrs. Armour sang. "Be ready when he comes, Oh, be ready when he comes. Jesus is comin' again so soon."

Mrs. Armour, who often is invited to sing spirituals in Madison-area churches, remembers that she sang on the train nearly every mile of the journey to Latonia, Kentucky, where she got a job as a cook at a racetrack to prepare dishes for the jockeys. "The racers come in there from everywhere—Florida, California, just everywhere," said Mrs. Armour, recalling that nine black and nine white women and two men worked in the kitchen.

"I'd go to work at five o'clock in the morning and have a rest period at two o'clock, and the races would start at three," she said.

Her boss, Mrs. Annie Slapp, allowed the kitchen staff to watch the races. "She'd let us go upstairs and look at them and clap our hands when the

Lucy Mae Armour sits on the front steps at her house and sings spirituals with messages about hope, faith and love. She remembers her mother sang spirituals from the heart and mind on a farm in Putnam County.

bugle would blow," Mrs. Armour said. "It was a great big porch, and we just would march from one end to the other by the bugle blowin'. I used to love to dance, and I'd prance when that bugle would blow. And the horses would prance by it."

She added, "The jockeys weren't any more higher than that [holding up her arm], little midgets, prettiest little things you ever seen, too pretty to be men. All called me Brownie."

Although her boss wouldn't permit the cooks to place bets on the horses, Mrs. Armor tried to pick the winners just for fun. "Oh, yes. I picked them things," she said. "Fair Play—that was the runnin'est horse you ever saw. She was poor, and she had a tail that wasn't more than that long. And she'd stick that little nub up and she could go. I saw her win races."

Mrs. Armour said some people make the same mistake picking horses and dogs at racetracks. "A lot of people go to these places and pick the fattest-looking horse and the fattest-looking dog up there," she said. "But that don't get it. You pick the poorest-looking old thing, and he looks like he can't hardly make it. That's your money."

Mrs. Armour was paid twenty-five dollars a week in salary and received tips from the jockeys, who slipped money under their plates to avoid being caught breaking the no-tipping rule. A jockey would stop and say, "'Brownie, whatcha pickin' today?' she said. "And I'd say my same horse. I'm gonna pick her till she stops racing. Old Fair Play'll bring you that money in the seventh race."

Clasping her hands, which have performed work for decades, Lucy Mae Armour says she was a cook at a horse-racing track in Kentucky during the 1920s. She danced when the bugle was blown, and racehorses would prance by the sound.

The jockeys were quite fond of her southern cooking, but they had to watch their diets and stay trim to race the horses, so they reluctantly declined seconds, she said.

Some of the horses, like people, had more energy than others. "You take myself," Mrs. Armour said. "A woman weighing 170 and 180 pounds, she can't run as fast as I do. I can get out right now and run way up yonder to the end of that road, and it won't make me too tired. I weigh 130 pounds, nothin' but my muscles."

On a Putnam County farm as a child, she wanted to go faster than the horse, so her mother made her climb down. "I'd get on a mule and ride back to the house, but I'd want to go faster," she said. "I'd try to plow and I'd walk faster than the mule. They stopped me from the mule and the horse."

Mrs. Armour remembers she got along fine with her boss and the seventeen other girls and knew love and friendship everywhere she went. "I never had a confusion [any trouble] the whole time I left Georgia," she said. "Whatever I told them or whatever they asked me to do, I did my best."

She returned to Georgia and was a cook for a number of years in a boardinghouse, cleaned a doctor's office, worked in a store and was a maid.

Her husband, Elmer, retired from a textile mill, and he has been ill recently.

She said someone noted the trouble with people today is that they have a "big hat or big head." Mrs. Armour said, "It isn't that. They don't have enough of God's spirit in 'em. God said for us to love one another and feel each other's care and help bear each other's burden."

Although poor and elderly, she is eager to help others when needed, and as long as she is able, Mrs. Armour will sing the praises of her Lord.

Singer Says Gangster Was Sweet, Courteous

GRIFFIN—A seventy-year-old Griffin woman who was a blues singer and dancer in the Prohibition era found Chicago gangster Al Capone much more appealing than silent screen star Rudolph Valentino. Although Mrs. Charlotte Sullivan never met Valentino, she had the thrill of being invited by Capone to join his party at a table after her nightclub performance one night.

She had heard a lot about "Scarface" but recalled that she wasn't nervous when introduced to him. "I met him and his brother," Mrs. Sullivan said. "Al Capone was one of the finest people to talk to. He was young and good looking. He reminded me of Al Jolson, in a way. He had a beautiful personality. Oh, Lord, yes, he was courteous to the ladies. He was one of the sweetest people I've ever known in my life."

She was making thirty-seven dollars a week singing, but when invited to go to a man's nightclub table or dance with him, she sometimes was tipped ten to twenty dollars.

"Everybody makes mistakes," she said. "Of course, he [Capone] was just terrible, from the things he did, or what I've been told he did. He was nice to me. He was a very sharp dresser and wore spats. He had manicured nails. The women were crazy about him."

Mrs. Sullivan recalled that Capone was witty and that he often told "cute jokes." She found him to be "more intelligent" than anyone whom she had ever met. "Everybody loved Al," she said. "He'd come in that club, and everybody wanted to shake hands with him."

Charlotte Sullivan of Griffin, a blues singer and dancer in the Prohibition era, said gangster Al Capone was witty and told "cute jokes." Capone was intelligent and a sharp dresser, and women were crazy about him, she recalls.

Mrs. Sullivan was born in Atlanta, and her father was a preacher who occasionally carried his ministry to jails. She got the show business bug after winning a contest in Atlanta singing "I Ain't Got Nobody" and "Am I Blue." She went to Detroit, answered an advertisement for a singer and landed a job in a nightclub.

Capone didn't ask her for a date, but his brother did, she said.

Mrs. Sullivan, who has been married twice and has been divorced about twenty-four years, said one request for a date nearly got her into trouble. "A man sent me a big batch of flowers every night, and I come to find out he was a member of the Purple Gang [in Detroit]," she said. "Yeah, I met him. Al Conn. No, I didn't go nowhere with him. My manager told me to watch it."

She once worked for a week as a burlesque dancer but quit for fear her father would hear about it.

Mae West was her favorite entertainer, and years ago, Mrs. Sullivan wrote her a letter saying she would like to walk in her shoes, but no reply ever came.

Reminiscing about dancing in her youth, Mrs. Sullivan said, "I could throw myself out of gear, you know." In doing the belly dance and other exotic dances, "you've got to have all the muscles relaxed and go. Can't anybody teach you anything. You gotta move everything."

Before becoming a dancer, however, she had to lose a lot of weight, trimming down from 208 pounds to a little over 100 pounds on her five-foot, one-and-a-half-inch frame.

She laughed in remembering how she held the end of her bed and learned to do the Charleston without a partner.

Referring again to Valentino, the idol of the silent movies, she said, "Honey, women fainted and fell over. He was south sea–like...South American. That's why he was like he was. They say any woman who went with him couldn't resist him."

Did she suppose he was as romantic off the screen? "That's what I wondered," Mrs. Sullivan said. "But, you know, to me...he wore those black patent leather shoes and all that stuff. But, shoot, Al Capone would attract me quicker than he would."

How does she feel about less emphasis being put on masculinity today? "Oh, Lord, just like a bunch of girls," Mrs. Sullivan said, "ain't they? But not all of them are. A long time ago, honey, a man was a man, and he got out and made that livin' for that gal."

When she was young, she noticed that lying was the most common fault in men, and they often said, "I love you" without meaning it. "I didn't pay no attention to it," she said. "It went in one ear and out the other. I guess I've been told that a thousand times. And I have told guys I loved them, but not in the way you would think. I love everybody. And that's all I've ever wanted—to be loved, needed and wanted. I think that's the three purposes of life. I've been needed all my life, and I'm pretty sure I've been loved."

Mrs. Sullivan said she has not been able to sing since someone strangled her, injuring her larynx, during an apparent robbery attempt as she slept during a visit in her daughter's home.

Two months ago she began accompanying her friend Gladys Whittington, manager of the hotel for the elderly where she lives, to the Southside Baptist Church.

Another fond memory of her youth was meeting singer Kate Smith, but it took a climb up a hotel fire escape to do it. Mrs. Sullivan and an exotic dancer friend were told by the hotel clerk that they couldn't go to Miss Smith's room, so they climbed a fire escape and knocked on her window. "She was very gracious," Mrs. Sullivan said. "We told her we were admirers of her. So she played a piano and sang a song for us."

Part III
Way Back When

Does Sign of Snake Point to Gold?

DULUTH—Joseph "Jay" Summerour hasn't ever bothered to hunt for the mythical pot of gold at the end of the rainbow. However, he hopes someday to find pots of gold nuggets that have been subjects of many legends since the white people forced the Cherokee Indians out of Georgia in 1838 on the infamous Trail of Tears.

Summerour, sixty and Duluth's postmaster, offered to take me in his four-wheel-drive pickup truck to the bank of the Chattahoochee River and show me two old beech trees that he believes were marked by Indians who left a trail leading to hidden treasure. The truck managed to make it through mud puddles, past red clay ditches and gullies and up slippery hills to the end of a road, where it then knocked down little pines and oaks on top of a ridge. He got out of the truck, walked across the ridge and then continued pushing through bushes and briars.

Suddenly, he stopped and asked, "Did you hear anything?" The only sounds had been our shoes crushing dry leaves and the wind murmuring in the trees.

"There used to be bears in this section years ago," he said. "I believe I could climb one of those trees if I had to."

Panting like a bird dog that is out of shape, I replied, "Yeah, I think I could, too."

I was already lost, so descendants of Indians who might have buried their treasures didn't have anything to worry about. Walking down the hill toward the river, I glanced back to the top of the ridge, already thinking of the trip back and regretting I'd gained weight in the winter.

Joseph "Jay" Summerour examines carvings that he believes Indians made on trees to mark a trail leading to buried gold. He has not yet found gold but believes about one hundred beech trees have carved symbols that will direct him to hidden treasure.

Summerour, who revealed he hadn't ever shown the Indian trail to any other outsiders, walked to a large beech tree, which he estimated could be two hundred years old, near the Chattahoochee's banks. "This is the sign of the snake on the bark," he said. "The Indians used a hand tool that we call a celt and, with this rock, bruised the bark very shallow so it healed over like this scar on my hand. It didn't hurt the tree."

Summerour explained that the snake, carved in a vertical pattern with its head at the top, was pointing to a tree on the other bank. He described it as a "pull tree," which Indians bent with thongs and stakes so that it aimed at the top of a hill. A few steps away from the snake symbol, Summerour showed me another very old beech tree with "one of the best drawings I have ever seen."

He interpreted the symbols on the bark to signify a cabin, an Indian's head with two feathers, two rabbits, a pot, an island, the confluence of two small streams, two arrowheads and a triangle with a hunting knife in the base.

Then he called my attention to an apparent message under the drawing. "We read this to mean, 'This is my grandfather, and this is his cabin, and I buried a pot [of gold] in the floor of his cabin,'" said Summerour. "This rabbit is probably telling us where it is. We think he is looking upstream on a creek to a little island where grandpa lived with plenty of water, fish and other food."

So far, Summerour hasn't found any pots of gold nuggets, but he is optimistic that the one hundred or more beech trees, presumably marked by Indians for trails, eventually will lead him to some treasure.

His old friend, the late Forest Wade of Forsyth County, who wrote about legendary Indian gold in his book, *Cry of the Eagle*, estimated that 98 percent of the buried treasure was dug up either by Indians soon after the turn of the century or by white people.

"All evidence shows that in 1909 a total of twenty-two wagons with eighty Indians came from Oklahoma and Arkansas to Georgia," said Summerour. "They had knowledge of what their parents and grandparents had told about the gold." He suspects the Indians went home with nearly $50 million in gold in wagons that left deep tracks later observed by white farmers, who had watched from a safe distance as the red men dug in the ground.

One of my fishing friends, Junior Collis, who was reared near Blue Ridge, was told by his grandfather that around 1909 Indians visited his farm, requested permission to camp and disappeared one night after digging a deep hole in a hillside. He, too, noted the wagon wheels left tracks indicating a heavy load.

Summerour believes signs that he interpreted on marked beeches indicate two trails to five pots of gold. "One was accidentally plowed up by a farmer years ago, two we believe are still in the ground and we believe the Indians got two others," he said.

According to one of the legends, Indians dug a tunnel and two-room cave near the Etowah River bank and then carved out niches for each family to leave treasure, sort of like modern-day safe deposit boxes, and covered each little opening with flat rocks. The legend is supported by markings on a beech tree that show a two-room cave, says Summerour, but the Cherokees warned of a trap—a large rock that would be triggered to fall and crush an uninformed treasure hunter at the entrance.

Summerour theorized that Indians didn't have any practical use for gold, which was too soft for arrowheads or tools, and they recognized its value only after Spanish explorer Hernando DeSoto and a band of about 250 men traveled from Tampa to North Georgia around 1541.

"They saw how anxious he was to get gold," said Summerour. "He came to get gold in the Appalachians. He saw some gold worn by Indians in Florida. DeSoto and his men may have left some gold in Georgia and left signs so they could pick it up on the way back to their boats. "

But the Spanish explorer died on the Mississippi River and was buried by his men before Indians could learn they had lost their leader, Summerour said. "I believe it was then that the Indians realized gold was a good medium for exchange, and for three hundred years they collected it, and each family built up a hoard," he said.

A big rock taken from the Frogtown area of Forsyth County to the University of Georgia was marked by Indians to show where thirty-two pots of gold were buried, according to Summerour, but he believes about twenty-five already have been dug up.

Everyone Can't Be a King

SAVANNAH—Several years ago, a man visited the Georgia Historical Society building and spent hours trying to learn more about his ancestors, who came here during the colonial period.

While reading an old newspaper, he suddenly burst into laughter.

Mrs. Lilla Hawes, then working with the society, asked, "What's the matter?"

He replied, "I've always been told that if you look for your ancestors long enough, you are going to find a horse thief. I found one."

Mrs. Hawes, sixty-eight, now retired, is rather amused that many folks spend a lot of time trying to find evidence of nobility in their ancestry. "I think too many people try to find their noble past and find out, if they go back to colonial America, most of the time it was humble beginnings," she said, "the people who really had the stuff in them to make it. To me, that is worth a great deal. There were some people who found a carpenter on their line and said that just couldn't be."

She was proud to learn that one of her ancestors was a successful blacksmith in South Carolina in the late 1600s and early 1700s. Another descendant of this blacksmith, however, wrote Mrs. Hawes and, obviously indignant, asked, "How dare you call my ancestor a blacksmith."

Mrs. Hawes said, "I don't know why these people have got these pretenses for nobility or aspirations toward nobility. Very few of us have those sorts of beginnings." She said the revered Nathanael Greene was a blacksmith as a young man and was proud of his experiences in that trade.

Mrs. Lilla Hawes, a history researcher in Savannah, finds it amusing that many persons spend a lot of time trying to find evidence of nobility in their ancestors, while most of the early settlers had rather humble beginnings in the Georgia colony founded by General James Oglethorpe.

Her favorite writer in the early years of Georgia's history was William Stephens, secretary of the colony's trustees, who wrote back to England providing detailed accounts of life in Savannah. "I think of him when we have cold weather in Savannah," she said, smiling. "He once wrote back home, 'It's been so cold here that even the chamber pot froze under the bed.' There was some kind of thing he wrote connected with some woman's corsets, but I don't remember. He wrote what was going on in every sphere… local gossip. That's why I love it so."

Mrs. Hawes said some modern-day black people in Georgia find it difficult to believe that in colonial days a few free blacks actually owned black slaves. She has read several bills of sale regarding such incidents and remembered reading the will of a free black woman who left her black slaves to someone in the family.

In one unusual case in central Georgia just before the Civil War, a black woman petitioned and received permission to sell herself back into slavery, Mrs. Hawes said, suggesting the woman might not have been able to make it on her own in those difficult times. "I am not condoning slavery," Mrs. Hawes said. "It was a horrible situation and should never have happened."

She reminded me that a few Indians also owned black slaves who were used as burden bearers.

Her husband, Foreman, now retired, was president of Armstrong College in Savannah. She spends her spare time on a special research project at the historical society in the W.B. Hodgson House.

Some of Georgia's so-called heroes had other sides that have been given little or no attention in history, lectures or textbooks. "Button Gwinnett was greatly revered as being a signer of the Declaration of Independence," Mrs. Hawes said. "I think he was as crooked as he could be—in his politics and other things, too. He had some shady financial dealings."

The more that she researches the life of General James Edward Oglethorpe, founder of the Georgia colony, the more she likes him. The first settlers in Savannah called him Father Oglethorpe and believed in their leader, whose motive probably was purely philanthropic, she said. Oglethorpe returned to England after the Battle of Bloody Marsh ten years after the colony was established and never set foot on Georgia soil again.

Mrs. Hawes said Oglethorpe "wasn't even in sympathy with the Americans' revolution" and that "the story about him being offered command of British forces in America is not true."

In Georgia's early years, Oglethorpe's birthday was celebrated, but then the practice lapsed. Mrs. Hawes said the *Georgia Gazette* announcement of his death was given a very tiny amount of space.

More Than a Fishing Village

DARIEN—A visitor from a big city sipped a cup of instant coffee in Darien City Hall and remarked that he liked "this quiet, quaint, friendly, little fishing village."

Darien's beloved, eighty-seven-year-old historian, Bessie Lewis, bristled, then broke into laughter and climbed onto her soapbox. Miss Lewis, who moved in 1912 from Ohio to nearby Pine Harbor, formerly known as Fair Hope, doesn't mind a city fellow thinking of historic Darien as being quiet or quaint or friendly, even little. But, by golly, don't make the mistake of calling this McIntosh County town of nearly two thousand "a fishing village."

Sure, the shrimp boats return to the Darien docks late each afternoon and the seafood industry pumps a lot of dollars into the local economy, but commercial fishing didn't get cranked up here until about 1900, she said.

Miss Lewis smiled and said, "Darien never was a fishing village, which I am fighting now. It never was a village. It's been a town, city, etc. We have our high bluffs here, and our vessels go out commercial fishing. Our blessing of the shrimp fleet is internationally known. It's never been a fishing village. It is a center for commercial fishing."

She added, "Darien has been a sophisticated town, and it has attracted travelers from many states and abroad. In the nineteenth century, a British and German consul were here. Men were playing golf in Darien in the 1890s."

Miss Lewis, author of a booklet entitled *They Called Their Town Darien*, emphasizes roles played also by naval stores, timber, agriculture, a shoe factory, local merchants and a bank that once was described as the strongest south of Philadelphia.

A shrimp boat returns to the docks at Darien, a town established in 1736 by Scottish Highlanders. Darien was known for naval stores, timber, agriculture, a shoe factory and a bank that was described as the strongest south of Philadelphia, said historian Bessie Lewis.

She wrote, "With all the changes and improvements there is something about the old town which remains the same. It is an indefinable atmosphere of friendly courtesy. One feels its old-time charm while still knowing the town is as modern as tomorrow. There are no strangers—though your face may be new, you are among friends. The town they called Darien, though like no other, will always be Darien."

Darien was established in 1736 by Scottish Highlanders recruited by General James Edward Oglethorpe, who three years earlier had founded the Georgia colony in Savannah. Between 1721 and 1727 at Fort King George near here, about 149 British troops had died of fever and malnutrition or in skirmishes with the Spaniards from Florida and the Indians.

Miss Lewis wonders what course Georgia's history might have taken if other early settlers had heeded the warning of eighteen bold citizens of Darien in 1739. A number of Savannah settlers had asked the colonial trustees to allow them to have slaves, and this became a controversial issue in the thirteenth colony.

John McIntosh Mohr, a Darien leader still grieving over the loss of his son, Lewis, killed by an alligator in the Altamaha River, called a citizens' meeting in his home. The document they drafted that January night in 1739 was not only bold but prophetic, observed Miss Lewis.

Eighteen Darien men strongly opposed importation of slaves from Africa, declaring:

> *It's shocking to human Nature that any Race of Mankind and their Posterity, should be sentenced to perpetual Slavery; nor in Justice can we think otherwise of it, that they are thrown amongst us to be our Scourge one Day or another for our Sins.*
>
> *And as Freedom to them must be as dear as to us, what a Scene of Horror must it bring about. And the longer it is unexecuted, the bloody Scene must be the greater.*

Again on January 12, 1775, members of a Darien citizens committee expressed their "disapprobation and abhorrence of the unnatural practice of Slavery in America."

Miss Lewis noted that this resolution was omitted by the Reverend George White in his *Historical Collections of Georgia* in 1854, although he reported that the committee had supported conduct of people in Boston and Massachusetts Bay in their conflict with the British Parliament.

Miss Lewis said Darien suffered greatly years later when Union troops burned the town in the Civil War and a black leader assumed control in the Reconstruction period.

In 1818, the Bank of Darien was founded on the present site of the St. Andrews Episcopal Church and set up branches in Savannah, Milledgeville, Augusta, Auraria and Marion. Some of the North Georgia gold mining operations were financed by the bank.

She said the bank was robbed twice and it "became involved in the bitterest kind of politics." She observed that notes it printed often "were in highest demand" but other times "were avoided like the plague." The bank suffered losses in the 1826 hurricane and a panic in 1837, finally closing its doors in 1842.

Miss Lewis, who writes a column in the *Darien News*, taught school for many years in Darien and McIntosh County. Her first teaching assignment was in a little yellow one-room school at U.S. 17 and Pine Harbor Road, attended by thirty students in grades one through seven.

She takes pride in the fact that the children did indeed learn to read with comprehension, unlike many modern-day Georgia kids, and they were taught to work and to assume responsibilities.

Living in the Style of the 1800s

CORK—The Hay sisters, Agnes and Vivian, were mighty glad to see cousin Ethel and her husband, L.J. Brown, from Jackson.

We were invited to sit on the porch of their five-room house that was built in 1893 by their father, Andrew Jackson Hay.

I was curious to see the inside of the old farmhouse, where the sisters, who are in their eighties, are living quite comfortably without benefit of such modern-day necessities as electricity, gas or running water, but the pleasant visit got no farther than the porch.

Sitting on an antique wooden chair, its high back held secure by strong cord, I had the eerie sensation that I was chatting with two women lost in time who were living in the style of the 1840s. Miss Agnes was wearing several layers of clothing, a jacket and laced boots, with a bandana wrapped around her head. Miss Vivian was in similar attire but also wore a long coat, and her head was protected by a crocheted wool stocking hat and a colorful bonnet. Her feet were kept warm in heavy socks and black work shoes.

The sisters lease part of their one-hundred-acre farm to hunters during deer season, and one of the men invariably stops here to tease Miss Agnes, who has quite a sense of humor and likes "to talk back to him."

One day, referring to an imaginary boyfriend, Miss Agnes told him, "Mr. C.J., I got me a new one."

"Who is that?" the hunter asked.

"He's just thirty years old," Miss Agnes replied. "And, I tell you, he doesn't chew tobacco. That suits me. He doesn't smoke. That suits me. He doesn't

Agnes Hay (left) and her sister, Vivian, made an Atlanta visitor feel as if he had stepped back into the 1800s in rural Georgia. They cook meals on a wood-burning stove and live in a house built in 1893 that has no electricity, gas or running water.

drink whiskey, and that just suits me. He doesn't gamble. That suits me. He cares nothin' about goin' fishin' all day, and that suits me."

The hunter asked, "Well, does he want to marry you?"

Miss Agnes said, "No, and that just suits me."

I asked her how such a lovely lady stayed single when so many eligible, handsome fellows in past years must have proposed to her. A smile spread across the wrinkled face, and her eyes twinkled, as she said, "I can tell you the truth. I had plenty of chances."

Way Back When

Many years ago, she told a cousin that she had fifty chances to get married, and he said, "Somebody's gonna say you is the biggest story teller in the county."

Miss Vivian, two years younger than her sister, suffered considerably from arthritis in the cold winter in the house that is heated only by fireplaces.

In a jocular vein, cousin Ethel's husband asked, "You slept with Arthur [arthritis] the past month, haven't you?"

She said, "Yes, I couldn't stand it. Got up in the mornin' and my legs wouldn't go. It affects my nerves and muscles. I get it in my neck, and it's hard to sleep."

Despite the aches and pains, Miss Vivian still cooks each day on a wood-burning stove or in nineteenth-century pots in the hearth. Miss Agnes helps in the kitchen but admits her sister is a better cook, and they share housekeeping chores.

Miss Vivian showed me the old, seventy-five-foot-deep well from which they draw a gallon of water many times each day for household needs and for their several cows. The trips to the barn per day are too numerous to count, says Miss Vivian, pointing out that a cow can drink five or six gallons of water without stopping.

Miss Vivian, who claims she's a better climber than her sister, goes up a ladder into the hayloft and uses a pitchfork to toss hay through the open door to cows patiently waiting for dinner.

She does little reading nowadays "on account of my eyes," but Miss Agnes reads aloud to her the news from the Jackson weekly paper, and they hear news on a transistor radio. Miss Vivian said, "She wants the weather on the radio, too."

Sometimes Miss Vivian looks out of the window and tells her sister, "I think you've got it out here now."

Miss Agnes milks their cows each day, and the sisters sell milk and home-churned butter to folks in this section of Butts County.

A friend or a relative takes the Hay sisters to a grocery store in Jackson every week or so, and in the summer they can a lot of fresh vegetables. Both sisters drink a large amount of milk, and they don't have to watch their diets. They work so hard that they never have weight problems. "I eat anything in the world that's made to eat and is good, except hot peppers," said Miss Agnes, "but don't you give me no hot peppers. They burn my stomach." Both sisters laughed when I told them that hot peppers made my scalp itch and caused me to break into a sweat.

Commenting on their lifestyle and showing me their kerosene lamps, Miss Agnes said, "We are antique. I am just as antique as I can be. I haven't got nothin' new. We haven't got no electricity. Tell you what I'd rather have electricity for. I'd rather have it for a washing machine and a Frigidaire.

Vivian Hay prepares to lower a bucket to draw water from a well at her farm home near Cork, Georgia. She carries gallon buckets of water for household needs several times a day and says a cow can drink five or six gallons at a time.

As far as the lights, that doesn't bother me."

Miss Agnes has watched television in a relative's home, but she isn't too impressed with the quality of programming. "I'm not missin' much, I tell you," she said. "Tell you what I'm missin', and I'm glad of it. It's those dirty things on television. And those crimes. Two boys the other day tried to wreck a train, and the police said, 'Where'd you learn this?' And they said, 'On television.'"

The Hay sisters are wary of strangers riding down their road because in 1973 they were robbed and beaten by two men who later were arrested, tried and convicted. Miss Agnes fears she looks even older than her years because one of the men knocked out several of her front teeth.

In their younger days, the Hay sisters enjoyed square dancing, and Miss Vivian was a rather skilled bowler. Miss Vivian also liked fast rides in a buggy pulled by a horse named Nellie. Neither sister ever learned to drive a car. The 1926 Model T Ford and the 1924 Ford touring car in which they rode with other family members are still stored in a barn and haven't been started since 1950.

It was almost time to start a fire in the wood stove and cook supper, so we said goodbye to these dear old ladies. Tomorrow would be another day of hard work, but they won't mind. Working just comes naturally to them.

Riding down the dirt road, I tried to think of a little gift to bring when I visit them again. I'll try to remember not to bring a jar of hot peppers.

Sermon Really Shook Them Up

PINE LOG—Back in the good old days in rural North Georgia, a Methodist preacher tried to put the fear of the Lord in the hearts of members of his congregation. If his impassioned warnings against stirring up the wrath of the Almighty hit the mark, then he went home, ate fried chicken for dinner and felt satisfied his flock wouldn't stray from the straight and narrow path in the coming week.

One preacher's prayer really shook up everybody here. The Reverend J.N. Sullivan received some quite unexpected assistance from Providence one hot day in the summer of 1886 in the Pine Log Methodist Church in Bartow County, fifteen miles north of Cartersville. People of all ages in the congregation were so shaken by the event of that historic day that modern-day members of the country church are still talking about the prayer that suddenly was answered by God.

Ben Maxwell, a farmer who lives in nearby Rydal, said his father, the late James Martin Maxwell, was a mighty frightened six-year-old boy on August 31, 1886. You can imagine how hot it must have been that day in the white frame church, which was established in 1834, as Reverend Sullivan preached in the annual Pine Log Methodist camp meeting. Members of the congregation probably were fanning their perspiring faces, and mothers were trying to keep their restless children still in the pews. Men sat on one side of the sanctuary and the ladies on the other side in those days.

Perhaps feeling that the folks sitting before him had grown a little lethargic and apathetic, the preacher decided he must arouse them so they would start working harder. Sullivan stood at the pulpit that memorable hour and

A preacher at Pine Log Methodist Church asked God to move the hearts of people in his congregation by shaking the ground, and his prayer was suddenly answered when tremors from the 1886 Charleston, South Carolina earthquake were felt in North Georgia.

prayed this prayer: "Lord, if it takes it to move the hearts of these people, shake the grounds on which this old building stands."

His prayer wasn't quite completed because, by an incredible coincidence, an earthquake at that moment struck Charleston, South Carolina, killing sixty persons and causing $23 million in property damages. Tremors also were felt considerably west of Charleston, including this rural section of Bartow County.

Maxwell, recalling his relatives' description of the earthquake, said, "Sullivan had a great response to his prayer. There was great fear and pandemonium. The mourners' bench near the pulpit was covered up with folks. I don't know if many ran out the front door. More of 'em went to the front to fall on their knees and pray."

I think it would be fair to conclude that everybody in the congregation felt at that moment that God was trying to tell them something.

Maxwell said that although the earth trembled in this area, the old wooden church building apparently wasn't damaged. "I understand it held up for several years and continued to be the subject of conversation," said Maxwell.

A marker in front of the church tells of Sullivan's prayer and the earthquake and includes this verse from the Book of James (5:16): "The effectual fervent prayer of a righteous man availeth much."

Old Houses from Genteel Era

MADISON—Visitors on tours of Madison every month of the year are delighted to discover that some of Georgia's most beautiful antebellum homes have been preserved and protected with pride. In this friendly, progressive Morgan County town, they also are happy to learn that the grace, charm and hospitality of antebellum Georgia are alive and doing well. The pace of everyday living is a bit slower than that of big cities. Folks you meet on the sidewalks take the time to not only chat with neighbors and show they care but also give visitors directions and welcome them to town.

Tours of Madison are conducted nearly every week of the year, but only twice are open house tours scheduled. You will have the opportunity to visit many of the lovely antebellum and late nineteenth-century houses. A northern tourist remarked last year, "This is so much more enjoyable than going to a museum because families are living in these gorgeous houses."

Joshua Hill, who served in the U.S. House and Senate and was a "staunch southern friend of the Union," was credited with preventing destruction of Madison by General William T. Sherman's torches on the infamous March to the Sea in the Civil War. County historian Caroline Hunt said that Hill, an acquaintance of Sherman's brother in Congress, met with Governor Joe Brown and the Union general after Atlanta's fall. They agreed upon a separate peace for Georgia, which Sherman hoped would make the whole Confederacy collapse without further bloodshed. Sherman promised that if the pact failed, he still would spare Madison.

Joshua Hill's white-columned home was built in Madison in 1842. Hill, who served in the U.S. House and Senate, was a staunch southern friend of the Union and was credited with persuading General William T. Sherman not to burn Madison in the Civil War.

Mrs. Hunt said a governor's aide informed Confederate president Jefferson Davis of the deal, and he persuaded Governor Brown to change his mind.

Fortunately, General Sherman honored his pledge to Hill, and Union troops left Madison unscarred except for the burning of the railroad station, an inactive cotton mill used as a prison for the Andrews Raiders and a doctor's medical books.

"Joshua Hill was a wonderful orator with a tongue that was honed on steel each morning," said Mrs. Hill, noting he had great ability and integrity but was an agnostic.

Mrs. Hunt said most visitors, especially those from the North, are eager to see fine examples of Greek Revival architecture. The houses must have big, white columns, like Scarlett O'Hara's Tara in *Gone With the Wind*. Many of them are found on Main Street, Old Post Road—an old stagecoach road—and Academy Street. Neighborhoods have changed quite slowly, and numerous old homes have been occupied by members of the same family for generations. These are among houses and other buildings that tourists find particularly appealing:

- **Joshua Hill's home:** Built in 1842 and remodeled in the 1920s, the picturesque, white-columned house would have been adored by Miss Scarlett and Rhett Butler.
- **President's House**: Actually it wasn't. It was constructed in 1849 and was the drama and art department of Georgia's Female College and was used as a hospital in the Civil War.
- **Boxwood**: The home of Miss Kittie Newton today, this was erected in 1851 and was one of Georgia's first prefabricated houses. The lumber was pre-cut in Augusta and hauled here on ox-drawn wagons.
- **Presbyterian church**: One of the state's prettiest houses of worship, it was constructed in 1841 and attended by Alexander Stephens and Mrs. Woodrow Wilson's father.
- **Heritage Hall**: Headquarters of the local historical society, this house was built by Dr. Roger Jones in the late 1830s and remodeled in the 1850s and 1880s. This, too, would have appealed to Miss Scarlett and her kinfolks.
- **Madison-Morgan Cultural Center**: Constructed in 1892, this two-story building was a school for many years. Visitors flock here to see exhibits of paintings, wardrobes of yesteryear, old-fashioned classrooms and other displays of nineteenth-century life.
- **Morgan County Courthouse**: A favorite of photographers, this striking structure constructed in 1906 was patterned after the Bulfinch building in Boston, a splendid example of early American architecture.

Wild Hogs Roamed in Mountains

BLAIRSVILLE—The North Georgia mountains were the home of many wild hogs when Will Davis was growing up on a farm close to Cooper Creek in Union County. His father, the late William Jackson Davis, hunted the hogs with dogs, and everyone in the family of nine was fond of the pork cooked on a wood stove.

"I guess it was a regular old domestic hog left out there by settlers when they moved out, and it went wild and got scrubbier," said Davis, fifty-nine, a wildlife technician and equipment operator in the Gainesville region of the Georgia Game and Fish Division.

"It's a long-nosed kind of hog, not too big, maybe 250 pounds, with big tusks. If you get in there in its bedding place, brush piles they'd build for sleeping quarters, you could very easily get attacked," he said. Davis heard years ago about a man who was knocked down by a wild hog and had his coat ripped off by the sharp tusks. A wild hog could kill a dog with one lick.

He and his brother-in-law, George Lyle, had a close call hunting wild hogs some years ago. Their dogs had a hog bayed, and the two men moved into the briar thicket for the kill. Davis was standing behind Lyle when the angry hog charged. "The hog didn't get more than ten feet before I shot him with my single-barrel, twelve-gauge shotgun," said Davis. "George said the shot didn't miss his leg more than six inches. He said, 'It's better to lose a leg than let a hog like that get you down.'"

The thought of facing a charging wild hog with a single-barrel shotgun in my hands gave me cold chills. I chatted with Will Davis, a tall, slender

Will Davis, who grew up on a farm in the North Georgia mountains, was known for working hard and being self-reliant with a deep understanding and respect for nature. "You don't lean on the other fellow too much for assistance," he said.

mountain man whose knowledge of plants, animals and the rugged wilderness has been invaluable to his boss, Hubert Handy, regional wildlife supervisor.

Davis's mother resides in a house near Cooper Creek on land that his great-grandfather, Billy Davis, homesteaded after moving to Georgia from North Carolina in the 1830s.

Walking in the forest near the house, Davis showed me a large, partially hollowed-out log that was used many years ago by his relatives as a tanning trough. The hole in the center of the old log now is filled with soil from decaying leaves, but the settlers used to put their cowhides in this cavity for a tanning process that required weeks.

A few steps up a trail in the forest lay a much older reminder of the pioneering days in North Georgia—a big rock that someone had never finished shaping for use in grinding corn. Deeply etched lines showed where the little depression or bowl would have been formed.

After meeting Davis, I understood what Handy meant when he called his friend "one of the last of a special breed of mountain men, hardworking, self-reliant, with a deep understanding and respect for nature."

Davis told me that one of the first things a man learns in growing up in the mountains is to stand on his own two feet. "You don't lean on the other fellow too much for assistance," he explained. "You learn to walk alone. You got to learn to be self-dependent. You don't depend too much on other folks. They won't give you nothin'. You got to earn your own way."

The quickest way for a fellow to lose the respect of his mountain neighbors was to tell a lie. "A man's word was his bond back then," said Davis. "His promise was good. There weren't many fellows who wouldn't come up to their promise. If they promised to pay you somethin', they paid you. The fellow who lied to his neighbor was just about the least thought of kind of character in the country."

The greed of modern men baffles Davis. "Ain't no use in bein' too greedy because a fellow ain't gonna take nothin' with him no how, you know," he observed.

He doesn't believe some folks in the mountains today are quite as neighborly as people were in his youth. "They don't visit like they used to," he said. "It's got to the point where it seems like each fellow is more to himself. And it's got to the point now if you visit some of your neighbors, they are in a hurry for you to be gone. They got somethin' on their mind and ain't got time to talk."

In his youth, people visited neighbors and offered help in times of illness and pitched in to aid a farmer who got behind on his crops. It wasn't unusual for a farmer with skill in carpentry to make a handsome coffin and offer it free to the family that lost a loved one and for neighbors to sit up all night with survivors during the wake. Back in those days before bodies were embalmed, a family's only expense was the burial clothes and a grave marker.

Davis remembers that he, his brother and their five sisters obeyed their parents and cheerfully performed a variety of chores in the house and on the farm. "They didn't tell it but about once, and next time they'd tear you up," he said. "Next time they told you to do somethin', you knowed what they were talkin' about. You wouldn't argue about it."

At Christmastime, few toys were under the tree, but kids appreciated what little they received. "If you found a nickel bar of candy or maybe an orange or apple, it was Christmas," said Davis. "It meant more than a Cadillac to some of 'em now. Mama made rag dolls, and my sisters were just as proud of 'em as children would be of a $100 doll now."

His father told the boys they could go fishing for trout on Cooper Creek and the Toccoa River over the weekend if they finished their farm work. "So, you worked pretty hard lookin' forward to Saturday evenin' gettin' that corn all hoed out," said Davis, who has baited his hooks countless times to catch rainbow trout for supper on a Saturday night.

The Davis children walked on a trail through the forest and across a mountain three miles to attend classes in a one-room school. "I've walked that trail as much as two weeks at a time with snow on the ground on the north side of the mountain," he said. "Ice was on the trees and bushes." In warmer weather, he saw deer and many squirrels in the unspoiled wilderness.

How did the Davis family learn news of the outside world? "We got a weekly newspaper, and maybe some of the neighbors would tell you about it a week or two later," he said. "You never stay up-to-date with the news unless it happened close by. It might be days and days before some of 'em even knew there'd been an election for president or who'd won."

Part IV
Exits

Destiny Halted Party for FDR

WARM SPRINGS—Framed on the wall behind Frank W. Allcorn Jr.'s desk is a print of an unfinished painting of a man who was his friend and neighbor. On the opposite wall is a large painting of the same distinguished gentleman as he appeared in 1936.

Allcorn admires the paintings each day and must wonder sometimes if the course of history might have been a little different had his good neighbor lived three more years to complete his important tasks. He also would have been interested to hear what subjects his friend had hinted he wished to discuss on what proved to be his final visit to Warm Springs. The man died before the painting could be completed of him posing next to the fireplace in his modestly furnished white cottage on the lower slopes of Pine Mountain.

Allcorn had arranged a party in honor of his old friend, President Franklin D. Roosevelt, at 4:30 p.m. on April 12, 1945. Guests had arrived fifteen minutes early as requested, but they didn't know the president had passed away at 3:35 p.m., two hours and twenty minutes after being stricken in the Little White House.

Allcorn, eighty-eight, a native of New York City and an Atlanta banker many years, vividly remembers the last time he saw FDR. After moving here in 1943, Allcorn renovated an old hotel and was elected mayor of Warm Springs.

> *I was asked by the head of the Secret Service to come to the train to meet him,"* said Allcorn. *"There was an elevator lift on his car* [Roosevelt contracted polio in 1921 at the age of thirty-nine and began visiting Warm Springs for treatment and therapy in 1924].

Retired Atlanta banker Frank W. Allcorn Jr. remembers guests arrived early for a Warm Springs party honoring President Franklin D. Roosevelt, and they were saddened to learn he had just died in the Little White House.

The car was called the Ferdinand Magellan and was the one he used most of the time he was president. He was closely protected in the war. That car had been made by the railroad people and sold to the U.S. government at a very nominal amount. Later, Truman and Eisenhower used it.

The war in Europe was grinding to an end in Germany, and battles for the Pacific islands were to continue until August, when atomic bombs were dropped on Japan.

"He didn't look as well as I had seen him," said Allcorn. "He had been through a terrible strain. But he was cheerful and said, 'I want to see you about certain things when I get settled down.' I was giving a party for him the afternoon he passed away. I had invited the White House group, and he had invited a number of local people."

A country band with FDR's favorite fiddlers from the Cove section near the Flint River was playing for the nearly eighty persons assembled. "The president had asked for the privilege of cutting the first piece of meat," said Allcorn. "He loved to carve meat."

Roosevelt was ten minutes late when Allcorn asked a White House communications officer if he knew why there was a delay on FDR's arrival. "He was a colonel. He said it happens sometimes when something special comes up in Washington."

United Press reporter Merriman Smith accompanied them to a short wave set, and Allcorn remembers him saying, "All I seem to be getting is a lot of double talk."

Allcorn continued, "He called up the White House operator here, and she said she thought it might be well for them to come down to her house."

Moments later, an announcement was made in Washington and Warm Springs that Roosevelt was dead.

In 1950, Allcorn became a member of the board of directors of the Franklin D. Roosevelt Warm Springs Memorial Commission, and since 1962, he has served as its executive director.

Last year, more than 139,000 people visited the Roosevelt Museum and toured the Little White House at Warm Springs.

Marines Called Oswald the "Creep"

WARNER ROBINS—A Warner Robins schoolteacher who served in the U.S. Marine Corps with Lee Harvey Oswald remembers him as an antisocial person whom fellow leathernecks dubbed "the creep."

Mrs. Michael Fitzpatrick, thirty-six, also has a vivid memory of the hot summer day in 1959 at the El Toro, California marine air station's rifle range when Oswald, despite the "devil winds" blowing sheets of sand from the desert, fired an M1 rifle with "fantastic accuracy" and astonishing rapidity.

She said, "I really believe he was physically and mentally capable of ripping off that many rounds in that amount of time" on November 22, 1963, when President John F. Kennedy was assassinated in Dallas.

Ironically, she had worked in Kennedy's senatorial campaign in Massachusetts and had met him and chatted briefly with him—first in 1952 and then again in 1958. She is now a social studies teacher at Sacred Heart Elementary School here.

As a young marine named Mary-Ann Perry from Warren, Massachusetts, who had recently received a history degree from Boston University, she went with fellow marines to the rifle range one day in 1959 to fire qualifying rounds. Mrs. Fitzpatrick remembers that everybody except Oswald was drinking coffee and talking while waiting for a lull in the windstorm before firing rifles at targets.

"He [Oswald] would be out there in the various positions: sitting position, prone, standing," she said. "He was out there ripping off rounds like you wouldn't believe. Rapid fire, everything."

The former Mary-Ann Perry reads the Warren Commission Report on the assassination of President John F. Kennedy. She served in the U.S. Marine Corps with Lee Harvey Oswald and saw him hit targets with a rifle at the firing range despite windy conditions.

Men in the pit crew, who raised and lowered targets and checked scores, also hadn't begun their work because of the strong winds.

"The weather was terrible, and no one else was firing," she said. "He still sat out there and would go from section to section. Of course, no one was pulling down the thing [target]. He would fire by himself, and he was good. He really was. We were fascinated watching him. He would finish and come back in."

Mrs. Fitzpatrick said he had "this self-satisfied look on his face. And, I thought, well, good for you. There's one thing you can do in this life. I can't think of anything else, but…"

"And he really looked very pleased with himself. He came in, and I said, 'Boy, you were fantastic. In this wind, how did you gauge the wind?' It would be a fantastic gust, and then it would stop."

She continued, "He was pleased as punch. I said I'm not going out there. Most of the fellows patted him on the back, and they said, 'Too bad this doesn't count for anything right now.'"

Mrs. Fitzpatrick would not even hazard a guess about the number of rounds Oswald fired in the estimated hour and a half of shooting from a range of about three hundred yards.

"He was very good," she said. "It was the thing he was really good at. And when you read some of the things they say he couldn't possibly have ripped off so many shots. That's foolish because he was really good at rapid fire. Let's face it. Any marine worth his salt, that's his first prerequisite. He's going to have to be a rifleman first."

She admitted she wasn't a very good shot with the rifle and remembers she thought that Oswald might give her some helpful hints. When she asked him how he did it, his reaction was, "I just can do it."

She was an air control officer in the main air control squadron—a small group—and Oswald was a radar technician. Mrs. Fitzpatrick said the squadron members worked "very long" hours under considerable pressure, and there was close camaraderie between the six persons on each shift.

A marine told her that Oswald was demoted to private first class while in Japan. "It was all hearsay," she remembers. "Someone said he supposedly had a Japanese girlfriend, and they were living off base, and someone of higher rank, who, of course, had more money, came in and stole her away from him. And he [Oswald] came back and proceeded to beat up the sergeant and the sergeant, of course, wasn't going to take that, and he put him on report."

She suspected that the only reason Oswald joined the marines was to gain some prestige in uniform that he never had received as a youth.

"He was a good radar technician," Mrs. Fitzpatrick said. "You couldn't take that away from him."

She saw Oswald for the first time when she was assigned duty as an air control officer and entered the small mess hall. The only female in the unit, she was introduced to the men, and they were friendly and treated her as someone "very important."

But, she said, "He [Oswald] came in, and he never looked up. It was kind of fascinating. It hurt my feelings terribly. I thought, how can you not look at me? I am standing here, the only female. He filled his tray, and there were about three tables in the shack. He went right to the end table, and he turned the little seat so he was facing the wall, and that was how he ate. I never saw him eat with us that he did not face the wall from the beginning of the summer until September."

She remembers the marines frequently tried to get a response from Oswald but admits that the marines were rude to him and continually harassed him.

Sometimes a couple of marines would walk to his table in the mess hall and announce they would eat with him, but Mrs. Fitzpatrick believes Oswald felt it was done merely to harass him. "Now that I am older and can see what youth could not see, we were rude to him," she admits. "He was an antisocial individual, but still there was no excuse for us to treat him that way."

A marine told her that Oswald sometimes would talk a little with the men in the barracks. She learned later that he subscribed to a Russian newspaper, although he could not read the language. She believes it was another effort of the young marine known as "the creep" to gain some attention and recognition of fellow leathernecks. Mrs. Fitzpatrick learned later that Oswald tried to enter the marines' foreign language school but was turned down.

She recalled that Oswald later was given a hardship discharge from the U.S. Marine Corps because he was the sole supporter of his mother.

When Oswald defected to the Soviet Union, Mrs. Fitzpatrick's air control squadron had to change frequencies immediately for security reasons. She said a marine, commenting after learning of Oswald's defection, said, "Poor Russia."

Mrs. Fitzpatrick said she felt ashamed of herself "for the way we treated him. But there was just something creepy about him. There really was. He would never look you in the eye," she said. She often has wondered whether "just one human act of kindness from any of us" could have "turned him" toward more normal behavior.

On November 22, 1963, her marine husband was on duty elsewhere, and Mrs. Fitzpatrick was with her mother in Massachusetts when they saw the television news accounts of the Kennedy assassination. Several hours later, she saw Oswald on television being escorted by sheriff's officers in Dallas. For a moment, the face looked rather familiar, "and then it hit me."

She recalled, "I said to mother, I know him. I was in the marines with him, but I can't think of his name now. Then they told his name."

Mrs. Fitzpatrick said, "I don't honestly think Russia had anything to do with it because I don't know of anyone who could really get to him, in him, enough. He would have to do something on his own."

Could Oswald have fired a foreign-made rifle of mediocre quality with such accuracy and speed to have killed Kennedy without a second gunman in another Dallas location assisting in the assassination? "Yes, I really believe he was physically and mentally capable of ripping off that many rounds in that amount of time, and as far as his capability as a marksman, yes," she said.

Mrs. Fitzpatrick first met John F. Kennedy when he ran for the Senate in 1952 and visited her hometown, Warren, Massachusetts, where she was an eighth-grade student licking stamps for his Democratic campaign.

She remembers that a local woman told Kennedy she had voted for his grandfather, who had sung "Sweet Adeline" to her, and the woman asked what he would do to get her vote. The Warner Robins housewife said, "He proceeded to go over to her, put his arm around her and he sang very loud and very off key the first verse of 'Sweet Adeline.'"

Kennedy stopped at the desk of young Mary-Ann Perry, impressed with an eighth grader's interest in his political campaign. He asked her name and hometown and briefly discussed her work.

Six years later, in 1958, Kennedy ran for reelection to the Senate and visited his headquarters in Boston, where Miss Perry was licking and stuffing envelopes again on his behalf. Kennedy walked past her desk and then suddenly stopped, turned and grinned, pointing his finger at her. "Warren, Massachusetts, Mary-Ann Perry, six years ago," Kennedy said.

She was astounded that he recognized her and remembered her name. "It was humorous," she remembers. "And he said, 'I never forget a name or a face.' I believed him. And he said, 'I guess I haven't been too bad. You still are supporting me.'"

She replied that in six years, she would be able to vote for him again if he sought reelection.

"And he thought that was hysterical," Mrs. Fitzgerald said. "He said, 'If I play my cards right, you may be able to vote for me before six years.'" At first it didn't dawn upon her that he possibly referred to a presidential bid in 1960.

She spotted him walking through the offices a couple more times in the 1958 senatorial campaign but didn't have another chance to chat with Kennedy.

In a strange twist of irony, the next year she was to meet a marine known as "the creep" who was destined to aim a rifle at John Fitzgerald Kennedy in Dallas.

Sylvia's Still the Talk of the Town

EATONTON—Perhaps the most fascinating woman in the history of Eatonton was a mysterious beauty known simply as Sylvia. Even today, half a century since she was last seen in the historic, white-columned Hunt house on Madison Avenue, Sylvia still is the talk of the town.

Several citizens told me:

- Sylvia's parents once lived in the three-story, twelve-room house that Henry Tripp was believed to have built in 1854.
- An out-of-state visitor in the Hunt house met her on the stairs, and it was a case of love at first sight. But it also proved to be the young man's last sight of her.
- She eloped with the town drunk on the day she was to have married a banker.
- Not so, another person says. She disappeared, but her skeleton was found in a big trunk in her room years after that day she was to have been wed.

Sylvia was quite a snooty creature who wouldn't be seen except in the presence of folks she considered to be her social equal. But there are two things on which believers in the Sylvia legend agree. Sylvia was absolutely beautiful, and she was a ghost.

Mr. and Mrs. James Liles have lived in the old Hunt house for twenty-five years, but neither has ever seen Sylvia. "Maybe it's because I am a non-believer," said Mrs. Liles, smiling. "I was aware of the story, and I had been knowing about the ghost since childhood. When we were children, we lived

According to legend in Eatonton, Georgia, beautiful and mysterious Sylvia, who has been seen several times through the years in this historic house, was believed to be the ghost of a woman who disappeared on her wedding day.

two miles from town and walked into Eatonton, but we would walk on the other side of this street. It was known as a ghost house and was vacant then."

Two persons speculated that Sylvia was the product of the imagination of Mrs. Benjamin W. Hunt, who reportedly saw the ghost several times between 1880 and the late 1920s. Benjamin Hunt was a prominent scientist and philanthropist from New York who married an Eatonton woman around 1876. He was credited with introducing Jersey cows in Putnam County and starting the dairy industry here.

One oft-told tale about Sylvia is that the late Mrs. Alice Wardwell, the city librarian, and some children were sitting on the library steps one day when they glanced across Madison Avenue and saw the female apparition in a front room in the Hunt house. Sylvia supposedly was looking over the shoulder of Hunt as he and his wife sat reading in the parlor.

A retired Eatonton lawyer, W.W. "Wink" Walker, once was told that a visitor to the Hunt home around the turn of the century briefly stood face to face with a lovely lady on the stairs. "It was instant love," said Walker. "After he left Eatonton, he wrote to Sylvia, and Mr. and Mrs. Hunt put the notes on the stairs. The next morning the notes always would be gone."

Walker also was told years ago that Sylvia was engaged to marry a local banker, although she still was in love with an Eatonton ne'er-do-well who couldn't leave booze alone. "On the wedding day, she asked the attendants to leave her alone in her room for a few minutes," said Walker. "She never came back out, and they had to break into the room. She was gone, and a window on the north side was open. They thought she had climbed down a rose trellis and assumed she ran away with the alcoholic. She left no note. That same day, the local ne'er-do-well also disappeared."

According to the same legend, the Hunts later bought the house, entered Sylvia's former room and found a large cedar chest by the window. "The story was that they found a skeleton in the cedar chest, and that Sylvia had lost her balance, fallen in, the lid closed and she smothered to death," said Walker.

While Walker was in high school in the mid-1920s, he went in the Hunt house one day to read the light meter for a local power company. He forgot his flashlight and had to prop the attic door open with a doorstop in order to see the meter. "The door closed on me," said Walker. "I opened it and the doorstop, twelve to fifteen inches tall, in the shape of a Negro mammy, was lying in the middle of the floor. The only other person in the house was the cook." Walker never learned who or what closed the door to the attic.

I wonder where Sylvia has been keeping herself all these years. Did she flee to the old tunnel beneath the Hunt house? No, I'm not going down there. That tunnel couldn't possibly be big enough for me and a snobbish ghost named Sylvia.

Haunted House Moans and Groans

SAVANNAH—A Savannah doctor and his wife hope the ghosts in their 181-year-old house will behave on Halloween night. But if the ghosts begin stirring around again, Dr. Clark Deriso and his wife, Melinda, probably won't be too surprised. After all, they reside in a beautiful home once described by a psychic researcher as "the most psychically possessed house in the nation."

While Mrs. Deriso and I talked in the den, the ghosts, to my sorrow, were polite and as quiet as mice. The only sounds we heard were natural—raindrops pattering on the roof.

She smiled and admitted being "horrified" upon hearing stories about Savannah's most famous haunted house before she and her husband bought it last year from Dr. and Mrs. Lawrence Lee. "I, to a certain degree, can see a very clear possibility the supernatural exists," said Melinda Deriso, who has enjoyed reading several books on the subject.

Is she still sometimes a bit afraid in the house at night? "Indeed I am," she said. "When my husband was in Dallas recently, I had friends stay with me and the children. I do not sleep a wink when he is out. I am chicken."

Dr. Deriso arrived home from his office and said he never has heard any ghosts, although shutters hitting the house in strong wind at night occasionally startle him. "The first time I heard shutters flapping in the wind, I almost jumped out of my skin," his wife said. "I have sat here on two occasions and heard what sounds like furniture being pulled across the parlor floor."

Perhaps the strangest thing that has happened since their purchase of the house involved a walk-in safe and the double doors leading to the backyard

This house was built in 1796 in Savannah by wealthy planter Hampton Lillibridge from Rhode Island. Doors leading to the patio and a walk-in safe's door were mysteriously opened, but nothing was disturbed or missing, owners said.

patio and rock garden. She was unable to close the safe door one day and called her neighbor, Betty Lee, former owner of the house, and requested assistance. The neighbor helped close the door and "locked the safe tighter than a drum."

The next morning, Mrs. Deriso checked on progress of the painters and discovered the safe's door was wide open. The painters said they arrived at

7:00 a.m. and discovered the patio doors were open, as was the combination-lock safe's door. Nothing was missing or disturbed.

It was further chilling for her to observe "pry marks" on the inside of the patio doors. The painting crew foreman had been given a key to that door. No other doors were open. The windows were nailed shut because the Derisos hadn't yet finished moving into the house.

"Dr. Lee had an incredible experience while living here," said Mrs. Deriso. "He isn't the type to make things up. He walked into the house one evening—his family had gone somewhere—and the phone was ringing. He answered it, and it was the answering service, and a patient needed a prescription refilled. He hung up the phone and went upstairs to their bedroom, and there was the extension phone receiver stretched across the bed—not on the nightstand—as if somebody had been listening. I don't know how to explain something like this."

The New England–style house with a gambrel roof and widow's walk rises three stories above a basement and has twelve rooms. The house was built in 1796 by a wealthy planter, Hampton Lillibridge, who had moved here from Rhode Island.

Jim Williams, a Savannah antiques dealer, bought the house in 1963, moved it from Bryant Street to 507 East St. Julian Street and restored the structure to its former splendor. That's when the ghosts began making nuisances of themselves.

Although Williams refused to discuss the haunted house with me—"I don't talk about that house anymore"—he was quite willing to tell reporters from Savannah and Atlanta newspapers about the ghosts and strange incidents in the 1960s. In 1964, Williams told an *Atlanta Journal and Constitution Magazine* reporter that while the house was being restored, brick masons ran frightened into the street after hearing strange footsteps, laughter, whispers and objects being knocked to the floor. A scared foreman was quoted as telling Williams, "That house is full of people that ain't working for you."

Williams told a Savannah reporter in 1967 about awakening around 3:30 a.m. and hearing footsteps near his bed making a sound like shoes on a sandy surface. "What do you want?" the frightened Williams asked. The intruder or ghost ran and bumped into an open closet door. After Williams slipped into the library and switched on a light, he still heard the footsteps. A moment later, he turned on the bedroom light but saw no one. The footsteps were heard no more that night.

Williams also told of three friends' strange experience in his home shortly before he returned from work one evening. They were startled when they heard noises upstairs, and one of them, a "strong athlete," went up the steps to investigate. Minutes later, they found their husky friend lying on his back on the floor and trembling with fear. The man had walked into the room and felt as if he had stepped into cold water, then was pulled by a mysterious force toward a thirty-foot-deep chimney shaft.

Shortly after the three men went to a friend's apartment across the street to wait for Williams to return, they heard a woman scream twice. Williams was quoted as saying the men ran into the street and saw a tall man with dark hair, wearing a white shirt and black bow tie standing at a third-floor window of the Hampton Lillibridge house.

Williams told a reporter that Dr. William G. Roll of the American Psychical Research Foundation stayed four nights in the house, trying to find anti-magnetic waves, caverns and underground streams. He quoted Dr. Roll as linking the weird happenings to "emotional waves," or vibrations, emitted by a body after a traumatic experience or death. Dr. Roll was quoted by Williams as calling the house "the most psychically possessed house in the nation."

Friends urged Williams to have the house exorcised, and he asked the Right Reverend Albert Rhett Stuart, then bishop of the Episcopal diocese of Georgia, to perform the ancient rite. Williams, a friend and workers doing the renovation watched on December 7, 1963, as Stuart blessed the building and prayed for removal of the evil forces. Only a few days later, however, workers sanding and varnishing floors heard strange noises again.

Two nights after moving into the house, Williams had heard "a kind of bellowing moan," and a few nights later he listened to "screaming, hollering and laughing" sounds on the top floor that made him "a nervous damned wreck." Another night a dark figure opened his bedroom door and then faded away.

Melinda Deriso was told that a woman who is a neighbor "on umpteen occasions has vividly seen a man in a tuxedo and top hat standing at a window and looking out." Another person recalled seeing two ghostly children on the parlor-level steps.

If Dr. Deriso and his wife had invited me to join them for a beverage Halloween night, I'd have replied, "Thanks, but I'm a chicken."

I think they would have understood.

Ghosts Slowly Floated Away

GREENSBORO—One morning, while making the bed in an upstairs room of her early nineteenth-century home, Carlene McCommons glanced at the mirror and saw the reflection of a little girl in the hall. She couldn't imagine who the child could be. Her husband, Roger, had taken their sons, Roger and Ross, and daughter, Rosalyn, to school.

"What I saw in the mirror was this little girl tiptoeing down the hall," said Mrs. McCommons. "I saw the back of her head. She had curls in her brown hair and wore a pink chiffon-looking thing."

She added, "I went into the hall and then every upstairs room. I couldn't find anybody. I thought, "This is the craziest thing I ever heard of." I went downstairs, and she wasn't there. She certainly was big enough for me to find her."

Finally, she concluded that the little girl of eleven or twelve who sort of "floated" down the hall was just one of the many ghosts that were occasionally seen and often heard by members of her family for twelve to fifteen years.

Deeta—her husband's nickname—and Carlene McCommons are quite intelligent, level-headed people who had never encountered any ghostly figures until they bought the three-story, Georgian-style house three miles west of Greensboro in 1959. The strange sightings and eerie sounds continued until about four years ago, when the couple completed extensive restoration work in the house. Since then, the ghosts have either floated elsewhere or just kept their mouths shut and their peculiar forms out of sight.

After the McCommons family began renovating this antebellum house near Greensboro, ghostly figures were seen on the porch, indoors in a chair and in the yard. Old-timey music, a child's reflection in mirror and the sound of a crying girl were quite unnerving.

"When we bought the house, it had been used for hay storage, and goats and cows had run around in it," said Mrs. McCommons. "I don't believe anybody had lived in it for twenty years."

She recalled, "It took us twelve or thirteen years to restore the house. We worked on it a lot ourselves and slept on cots and built a fire in the fireplace and camped out. We cleaned it up, knocked down crumbling, broken plaster in the hall and bedrooms. While we were working, it got messy. We got a feeling of oppression and depression in the house. It was kind of like somebody didn't like you. Once it started shaping up and looking better in the house, the feeling would go away." She said it made them wonder if somebody wanted to do something to the house and couldn't years ago.

The house was built around 1825 or 1830 by Joel Early, whose brother, Peter Early, was elected governor of Georgia in 1813. Mrs. McCommons said Joel Early lived in the house and died in 1852, and his widow, Grace, continued residing there during the Civil War.

Mrs. McCommons said old-timers had described the house as being haunted, and tales were told of chained men walking down the stairs at night or a peg-legged person pacing on the third floor. A man who said he lived in the house in the 1920s visited them and asked, "Is that old peg-legged man still around here?" Deeta McCommons replied, "Yes, he is still here."

McCommons said he and his wife were awakened by numerous strange sounds, including "Old Peg Leg walking up there." They would try to laugh and go back to sleep. I can imagine that wasn't easy.

One night after hearing of a tornado watch in this area. McCommons stepped to a second-floor window to check the sky and saw "a ghost walking in the backyard." He called his wife to the window, and she, too, saw "a form kind of floating along in the yard."

Then their daughter, Rosalyn, said she was afraid to go to the third-floor storage area to get her doll because "someone walked behind me." No, it wasn't the echo of her own footsteps, she said. Mrs. McCommons remembers her daughter saying, "I know what an echo is. When I stopped walking, whatever it was just kept on walking."

When Ross was quite young, he told his parents of seeing "a little boy upstairs," and he pleaded with his mother and father not to go up there.

As the three children grew older, they learned to laugh at the strange sounds and, while studying, even had the nerve to tell a ghost, "Please shut up. Get out of here so I can study."

One summer night when Roger was a child, he invited a boy from his school class to spend the night in a tent in the front yard at Ducaro, which the house had been named. About 2:30 a.m., his little friend peeped out of the tent and saw an old man rocking in a chair on the front porch. Roger also saw the figure. He advised his friend to go to sleep, explaining, "It must be a ghost. We don't even have a rocking chair on our porch."

Mrs. McCommons said that Rosalyn saw a ghost late one afternoon while she was studying in an upstairs sitting room adjoining her bedroom. "She reached up to turn on the lamp and looked in her room and saw someone who looked like Daniel Boone, wearing rawhide with a long gun in his lap, sitting in the chair," said Mrs. McCommons.

At first she thought it was one of her brothers playing a prank, and she resumed her studies, but a moment later she looked up, and the "pioneer" figure was still in the chair. She walked toward the door, and the figure faded away. Minutes later, Mrs. McCommons examined the chair and observed "a perfect imprint where someone had sat in the chair that I had smoothed out that morning."

While making jelly one day in her kitchen, Mrs. McCommons thought she heard her daughter singing and humming upstairs. She called her three times, but Rosalyn didn't answer. "Deeta came in from the chicken house, and I told him I called but she wouldn't come," she said. "He said Rosalyn had been in the chicken house working with him an hour and a half. She was not in the house. Nobody was in the house but me."

Another day, while upstairs, Deeta heard an old-timey kind of music coming through the heat vent, and he later told his wife he liked the music on her radio in the kitchen. She looked surprised and informed him she hadn't turned on the radio or the television set.

Mrs. McCommons recalled the night that Roger couldn't go to sleep because he heard his sister crying in her room. "He kept hearing her crying, and she finally was crying so loud that he went to the door to see what was wrong," she said. "He looked in, and she wasn't in the bed. He then remembered she was spending the night away from home."

The boy walked downstairs to see whether it was his mother's crying that he heard. His parents were fast asleep in their room. The crying girl was added to the long list of ghosts at Ducaro (a word formed from the McCommons family members' names).

Mrs. McCommons thought it might be interesting to invite a palm reader and adviser to the house and ask her for explanations of these ghostly matters. The visitor said she had a feeling a little girl had died after falling from a swing many years ago, and suddenly she pointed to an old tree in the pasture, saying this was where it happened.

Mrs. McCommons found this statement rather chilling, because fifteen years earlier she and her husband had inspected the grounds of their recently purchased home and found two old chains high in the tree on a big limb that had grown around the links. Her husband had observed at the time that this must have been a child's swing many years earlier.

The only other chains that possibly figured in the house's history might have been around the ankles of "bad slaves" locked in a basement cell that had a big steel door and large, wooden lock, according to McCommons. Perhaps it was their ghosts whose chains rattled on the stairs. McCommons said, "Joel Early freed his slaves early and offered them passage to Liberia."

She is glad that the ghosts finally approved of the vast improvements made in the old house. The ghosts had been hanging around long enough, and it was time to turn the house over to the present owners.

Church Booted Straying Members

APPLING—Baptists in Georgia in the late 1700s and early 1800s kicked out church members who strayed far off the straight and narrow. I suspect the preachers are sort of glad that the churches don't hold monthly trials nowadays in the Peach State. Otherwise, they'd be staring from their pulpits at a number of empty seats each Sunday morning. I can imagine some folks would be excommunicated after being found guilty of such charges as:

- Oversleeping on Sunday after watching the late, late show on television.
- Going fishing or playing golf on the Sabbath Day.
- Cussing out the deacon who sold a used car that was a lemon.
- Being spotted looking with obvious lust at the curvaceous wife of the chairman of the ushers committee.
- Daring to drink bourbon and branch water in one's own home, or anywhere, for that matter.
- Gossiping with the girls in the beauty parlor.
- Betting on a football game.
- Telling the Internal Revenue Service to catch the next jet plane to hell.
- Suggesting that they start serving burgundy or pink Chablis instead of grape juice at the Lord's Supper.

These charges may sound a bit farfetched, but back in the 1790s the Georgia Baptists wouldn't tolerate any minor or major sins among members of the flock. In Appling, the Columbia County village that also is the county seat,

G.B. Pollard reads 1790s conference minutes about disciplinary actions at Kiokee Baptist Church. A member found guilty of a sin could be kicked out unless he or she confessed, promised to be good and pleaded for restoration to full fellowship.

I read some of the Kiokee Baptist Church's monthly conference minutes describing disciplinary actions in those early years.

The Kiokee church was established in 1772 by a Connecticut Yankee, the Reverend Daniel Marshall, and was Georgia's first Baptist house of worship.

A member accused of a sin was brought before the conference and kicked out, if found guilty, unless he or she confessed, promised to be good and pleaded for restoration to "full fellowship."

In 1791, a man was booted for being intoxicated, and another was dropped from the rolls "for infamous language against the church of Christ in the courtyard."

The Baptist leaders decided it was "a crime" if a member failed to attend the monthly meetings and stated they "feel it our duty to warn such of this great evil."

A woman was expelled for "whoredom," and a man confessed he had been fighting with another fellow.

A man was kicked out "for leaving his wife and taking another woman."

A woman was accused of disobeying the church, and a man was expelled in 1793 "for the horrid sin of slandering the church of God and accusing it with partiality and likewise accusing the chairman of falsity."

In 1795, a woman was accused of dancing—a deep, dark sin in those days—and a man in 1796 was charged with "not letting his wife live with him in peace and trust and for having dancing in his house."

Another man, apparently a merchant, was accused of "keeping open doors on the Sabbath" in 1798.

One of the female members was taken off the church rolls "for rough expressions" in 1799, and the same year a woman was charged with "ill treatment of her husband."

I couldn't help but wonder if she hit him on the head with a frying pan.

Old Dan Tucker

HEARDMONT—A tourist taking in the noteworthy sights of Elbert County is likely to be asked, "Want to see old Dan Tucker's grave?"

Don't feel like the Lone Ranger if you reply, "Dan who?"

For a moment, the name didn't ring a bell to me either. Then someone reminded me that he was a soldier in the American Revolution (on our side, fortunately), a plantation owner, a ferryman and a preacher.

Still no bell was ringing.

Then I recognized the name as someone recited one of the dozens of verses written and sung over the years about the interesting character:

> *Old Dan Tucker was a grand old man,*
> *He washed his face in the frying pan,*
> *He combed his hair with a wagon wheel,*
> *And died with the toothache in his heel.*

Robert L. Williford, editor and publisher of the *Elberton Star*, directed me along a red clay road near the Savannah River, and we stopped at a granite marker that informs wilderness tourists they are near old Dan Tucker's grave. Walking up a narrow, well-worn, eroded path past bushes and small trees, Williford and I watched the ground just in case some copperheads were touring the area, too. We reached the hilltop cemetery in the peaceful, beautiful forest and saw a number of simple tombstones, some little more than knee high, with rather crudely carved letters and dates.

The Reverend Daniel Tucker, remembered in song as "old Dan Tucker," was buried in 1818 near Elberton. Black slaves welcomed him on visits to plantations and were credited with the song that became part of American folk music. His own plantation was named Point Lookout.

On old Dan's grave marker, I read, "To the Memory of the Rev. Daniel Tucker, Born February the 13, 1740, DP [departed] This life April the 7, 1818."

"Do you hear the river?" Williford asked. "That's Cherokee Shoals. This used to be the old homesite, and this used to be called Tucker's Ferry." Tucker's plantation, which afforded a picturesque view of the Savannah River, was named Point Lookout.

As we stood on the shaded hill listening to the river breaking in the shoals, I yearned to hear the voices of black men and women on a Georgia plantation singing a verse such as:

Old Dan Tucker, he got drunk
He fell in the fire and kicked up a chunk,
A coal of fire got in his shoes,
And, oh, my Lord, how the ashes flew.

A few minutes later in Elberton, Williford showed me a book entitled *Georgia Scribe*, written by Herbert Wilcox, eighty-five, a former *Atlanta Journal* state news correspondent and Elberton reporter who devoted part of a chapter to Dan Tucker.

Wilcox said the late Mrs. Guy Rucker, great-granddaughter of a neighbor of Tucker who also served with him in the Revolutionary War, described old Dan as "a minister who felt a deep responsibility toward the Negro slaves" and spent a lot of time "praying with the slaves and instructing them in religious matters."

Plantation owners enjoyed the preacher's visits, but perhaps even warmer welcomes were given by the slaves. "The Negroes adored him, and Mrs. Rucker said that it was they who started the famous song that is a part of American folk music," wrote Wilcox in his book.

"Nobody knows how many verses there were nor how many there are now because new ones are being added even today. The chorus about 'You're too late to get any supper' was probably sung by teasing Negroes who saw him ride up after supper was over and then hustled around to stir up a belated meal for him."

It's improbable that old Dan Tucker "got drunk," but in that day ministers enjoyed a toddy. And he didn't die with a toothache in the heel.

But if old Dan could stand on the Savannah River bank again today, he undoubtedly would be as pleased as punch to know the verses about him are still drawing laughs in 1977. He wouldn't mind if you sang a verse and chuckled right in front of the tombstone.

Farewell and Good Luck

MADISON—Most folks don't give any thought to the kinds of epitaphs they would like on their tombstones. I think they are just hoping for the best.

A friend in South Georgia would be content with the message, "Good luck."

Another fishing buddy probably would like this thought: "May you have tight lines and bent fishing poles throughout eternity."

Someone else would be pleased with, "May they always be biting on that distant shore."

However, one's favorite pastime rarely, if ever, is mentioned on a tombstone. It's not uncommon, though, to find a design indicating his or her profession, such as a scroll for an educator or an open Bible for a preacher.

On a very cloudy, windy afternoon—not what you'd call cheerful weather—I strolled through the oldest section of the cemetery in Madison, a town that was established in 1809. Some of the Madison pioneers buried here were born in England, Ireland and Scotland in the late 1700s and early 1800s. A number of Confederate soldiers were laid to rest here, some with handsome tombstones bearing epitaphs, others with plain markers.

Many slaves are lying in unmarked graves, which are noticed only because of sunken or recessed areas of earth now covered by grass. Most of the epitaphs on the old tombstones are Bible verses, lines of affectionate poetry, brief expressions of love or a few words of praise.

The inscription on the tombstone of one man (1829–1905) reads, "A brave Confederate soldier whose love for Dixie was second only to his love for God."

A woman who died at age twenty-three in 1897 inspired this thought: "Day after day, we think what she is doing in those bright realms of air."

A worker mows grass in the oldest section of the Madison cemetery. Some Confederate soldiers and early settlers born in England, Ireland and Scotland in the late 1700s and early 1800s are buried in the town that was established in 1809.

The 1905 grave marker of another woman was inscribed with the words, "She hath done what she could."

One of the best-known Madison citizens buried here was Joshua Hill (1810–1891), who served in the U.S. House of Representatives and the Senate and twice was a delegate to Georgia's constitutional convention. The epitaph described him as a "staunch Southern friend of the Union."

The tribute to his wife, Emily, reads, "As one candle lights another, so nobleness enkindleth nobleness."

A gentle shower was falling when I paused at a grave marker for a woman who died in 1871 and read the tribute: "Oh, mother, dear, a short farewell, that we may meet again above, and rove where angels love to dwell, where trees of life bear fruits of love."

Among the other epitaphs were:

"May the Lord have mercy upon her soul."

"He was the sunshine of our home."

"Here I lay my burden down, change the cross into the crown."

"In my hand no price I bring, simply to thy cross I cling."

"Gone to a bright home where grief can not come."

"Prophet" Prepares for Eternity

ON A COUNTRY ROAD—Several miles south of Madison off U.S. 441, a rough dirt road winds through the woods to the farm home of an old man who spends each day preparing for Judgment Day. William "Prophet" Kitchens, seventy-six, keeps several fence posts painted white, hoping they will be noticed if an angel of the Lord happens to be passing through this corner of Morgan County. Nailed to the trunk of an old oak tree in his yard is a crudely lettered sign bearing the message, "God is just a step away, prays [*sic*] the Lord, think [*sic*] you Jesus."

A young woman appears at the door of the unpainted wooden house with a tin roof and no electricity, running water or indoor plumbing and says her father is working in the family cemetery. It has become the daily custom of the slender black man to work on simple benches, a table, religious symbols and his own grave site near the cool spring that he believes his father, Oscar, found one hundred years ago.

Kitchens shows me where he wishes his body to be laid to rest. The area is marked by a rectangular pattern of metal posts, pipe and uncoiled springs, all painted white. "I'll be by myself there," he said. "You can't put two bodies in this grave." He indicates that his wife, Mary Lizzie, fifty-one, and their eight children will be buried at other sites near this metal-framed grave.

Some other fence posts are painted white in this area, and auto hubcaps and tin pans are hanging from tree trunks. This whole project on the eighty-five-acre farm is intended to represent a scene that he says he saw in a dream. "I dreamed about it," said Kitchens. "See that hill over yonder and

William "Prophet" Kitchens has placed a variety of objects at his planned grave site. He painted several fence posts white in hopes that an angel of the Lord will notice them if one happens to pass through the rural area.

the marks on trees? In the dream, they had lights on trees. It looked like a beautiful city. God had me come here and make this cemetery. In the dream, the cool spring down there had lights around it. The white posts are signs for angels to see. I believe all this is appealing to Jesus Christ."

Kitchens believes that his mother and father, who died many years ago, appeared in a dream to see how he has been getting along on Earth. The old man feels that Judgment Day will come sooner than many folks might suspect.

"We are getting close to Judgment Day," said Kitchens. "The world has changed so much. Jesus is coming back. The world is so full of sin, so much sin. Young couples don't believe in this. If it is a liquor joint or beer saloon, though, it would be crowded. Young people say they don't have time to talk about God. Both women and men are getting wicked."

He said the church that he attended did not believe in the project to which he devotes each day, but he is not discouraged, and he softly sings an old hymn: "Lord, lead me…wherever I go…lead me…stand with me. God does it…up and down the highway, I pray…God understands me."

Kitchens believes that one morning, soon after sunrise, when he walked to the spring to pray, he saw an angel fly back and forth in the sky, playing a guitar and singing, "Just look...just think...what is William Kitchens leaving behind?"

I wondered what he figured heaven would be like. "You'll be saved," he said, looking at the blue sky and scattered clouds. "Ain't gonna be nothin' but joy, joy, joy. No more hard work. No more taxes and bills. Just love in eternity with God and Jesus Christ."

Kitchens showed me three metal rings or hoops that he nailed in two trees under a frame in which he will put a painting of Mary and the baby Jesus. He explained a couple would step through the rings before facing a preacher in a marriage ceremony. I believe such rings were used in ancient rites by inhabitants of Caribbean islands.

Kitchens smiled when I remarked that it reminded me of a couple hopping over a broom and accepting each other as lifetime partners. "Yes, put the brush broom down and jump over it," he said. "That's what they said a long time ago in the country. Glad you heard it."

I observed that some troubled couples today probably wished they could jump backward over the broom. The old man, a look of sadness now in his eyes, declared, "Some young people ain't no count today. Can't make 'em work. They're so disobedient. They just want to frolic all the time."

He advised, "Pray and get God in your heart. The end is gettin' closer."

Part V

Side Trips

Is It the Coca-Cola Recipe?

GAINESVILLE—Is it the "Real Thing"? By golly, is this the recipe for "the pause that refreshes"?

While sipping a canned Pepsi-Cola in a Gainesville drugstore, I waited for a fishing friend to guess the answer.

"I believe it is," said pharmacist Everett Beal, as we read ingredients to make what a druggist more than fifty years ago identified as "Coco [*sic*] Cola Improved."

The formula for a soft drink had been written in brown ink on two pages of an old book of "receipts"—the old-fashioned word for recipes—owned many years ago by a Georgia pharmacist. After his death, the book was given to another druggist, whose widow years later gave it to Everett, who then was operating a drugstore in Griffin.

Just as confident as I am that the sun will rise again in the east tomorrow, I'll bet Everett and I never will know whether the recipe actually was an early Coca-Cola formula.

Only two, perhaps four people on planet Earth know the complete Coca-Cola recipe, and their identities are a very closely guarded secret, I'm told, "for obvious reasons." I wonder whether they ever talk in their sleep.

Everett and his wife, Judy, haven't tried yet to mix any "spike" or "dope." Those were nicknames my late grandfather and other old-timers gave to the new-fangled drink advertised as Coca-Cola decades ago.

Even if this were a fifty- or seventy-year-old Coke formula, I'll bet ingredients for the "real thing" are slightly different today. Some of the things listed on pages 188 and 189 in the old book of receipts would be hard to find. Federal

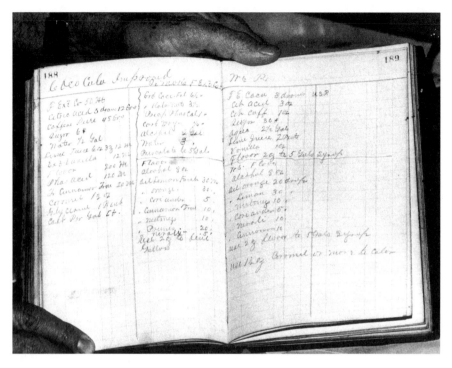

This recipe for a soft drink appeared in an old book of "receipts" owned by a Georgia pharmacist. Ingredients included ground coca, alcohol, nutmeg, prunes, cinnamon, caramel, sugar, water, citric acid, vanilla extract, lime juice, lemons, oranges and caffeine.

agents might frown if we went shopping for ground coca or fluid extract coca. Cocaine is among several things extracted from leaves of a tropical plant called coca. We easily could find alcohol, nutmeg, prunes, cinnamon, caramel, sugar, water, citric acid, vanilla extract, lime juice, lemons, oranges and caffeine. Maybe there's a grocery store special this week on cola nuts shipped from Africa. Seeds or nuts from this African tree contain caffeine.

The Coca-Cola Co. says the "birth of a refreshing idea" occurred in Atlanta in 1886 when pharmacist John S. Pemberton, "according to legend, first produced the syrup for Coca-Cola in a three-legged pot in his back yard." His bookkeeper, Frank M. Robinson, suggested the name.

The *Atlanta Journal* on May 29, 1886, published a small advertisement hailing Coca-Cola as "delicious, refreshing, exhilarating, invigorating."

Coca-Cola was described as a "new and popular fountain drink, containing the properties of the wonderful coca plant and the famous cola nuts."

On a sunny, cold morning in Atlanta, I took a photograph of the old soft drink formula to the office of Bill Pruett, public relations director of the

Coca-Cola Co. Dashing toward the goal line right away, I asked, "Bill, how many people in the world today know the Coca-Cola formula?"

Pruett, commendably composed, said, "I don't know...The precise information about what individuals by name at any given time know the full recipe or formula for Coca-Cola is something that simply isn't discussed here."

I had figured it wasn't bandied about during the morning coffee and Coke breaks.

Pruett said that probably "no more than a couple of people" in the company know the full formula. Two retired people likely had knowledge of it.

I told Pruett about seeing the old book of receipts, placed the photograph on his desk and asked, "As you people say, is this the real thing?"

He chuckled and said, "Well, you know I'm interested in looking at it... but I couldn't conceivably tell you."

Through the years, numerous people have claimed to have the original Coke formula, requested a confirmation or denial of authenticity or offered to sell it to the company.

The Coca-Cola formula is a "proprietary secret" that is "technically" unknown to the federal government, although the company must certify that Coke contains or does not contain certain elements.

Pruett said the company has gone to court a number of times to protect its name and trademarks.

"The position we have taken in modern years is that we don't as a company comment on or confirm or deny any information you present to us about the formula for Coca-Cola," he said.

I left the photograph with Pruett and had a hunch that it would either raise some eyebrows or make somebody chuckle up yonder in the executive suites.

And it isn't likely that I'll ever know if it was the real thing.

How Old Coke Became New Coke News

By Chuck Salter

The previous column and the accompanying photo of what may be the original recipe for Coke made quite a splash. International news, in fact. But it took thirty-two years for that to happen.

When the story first appeared in the *Atlanta Journal-Constitution* in 1979, Coke's hometown paper didn't put it on the front page. Or even on the front of the local news section. The piece and the list of ingredients for "Coco-Cola Improved" ran on page 2B. Papers around the globe didn't clamor to run the story. This was before the Internet, before cable news. CNN wouldn't launch for another year. So, the Coke column remained simply a personal favorite for my dad.

Fast-forward three decades. In 2010, Ira Glass, the host of the popular public radio show *This American Life*, read the column and eagerly reopened this colorful chapter in Coke's history. My wife, Lisa Pollak, a producer at the show, shared my dad's columns with the staff for a potential story, which ultimately became an episode called "Georgia Rambler." Various writers and producers, myself included, traveled to Georgia as modern-day Ramblers and did stories about the people we encountered. The column about Coke wasn't mentioned. Glass saved it for another show, "Original Recipe."

Like my dad, he was intrigued by the possibility that he was looking at one of the most closely guarded trade secrets in the history of American business. Glass suggested, What if you put the recipe in the photo to the test? What if you made it and compared it to the real thing?

A 125-year-old recipe is not something you just whip up in the kitchen. Modern flavoring technology has changed; thirty drops of nineteenth-

The beverage in this bottle was mixed by chemists at the request of Ira Glass, director of the public radio show *This American Life*, who said it tasted like Coca-Cola. Chemists used ingredients seen in a 1979 photo that Charles Salter made of a possible early Coca-Cola syrup recipe.

century lemon oil is nothing like thirty drops of twenty-first-century lemon oil. And coca, one of the key ingredients, doesn't have the same kick. Originally, it contained cocaine, but starting in 1903, Coca-Cola decocainized the coca leaves. Nonetheless, Glass and producer Ben Calhoun worked with Jones Soda and its flavor partner, a company called Sovereign Flavors, to produce bottles of "Coco-Cola Improved," taking into account the technological changes.

Along the way, *This American Life* also compared the formula to one in Coke's own archives. It was in a notebook that belonged to John Pemberton, the pharmacist who invented Coke. The two formulations are virtually identical, except that the one that my dad wrote about included the ingredient amounts. It was written in a pharmacy recipe book believed to belong to a friend of Pemberton's.

As for the taste test between *This American Life*'s soda and modern-day Coke, regular Coke drinkers could tell the difference. But some of the corporate flavor experts couldn't. Based on his research, Glass concluded that the formula was one of the original recipes—a precursor to what went to market, a later improvement or, yes, the actual recipe.

In February 2011, the radio story aired and exploded like a soda can that had been rolling around in the back of a car. *This American Life*'s website crashed from the traffic surge. "Our website has never gone down," Glass told a reporter. "We're the biggest podcast in the country and we're used to a lot of traffic."

Thanks to the Internet, the story went viral. An early piece on the *Today Show*'s site rippled overseas to media outlets in Australia, and the news spread to Russia, India, China and the UK. Throughout the week, the *New York Times*, CNN, ABC, CBS and Al Jazeera rushed to do stories. Conan O'Brien joked about it in his monologue. This time around, the *Atlanta Journal-Constitution* put the Coke story on the front page. The Coke news became one of the top ten items on Google News, with more than three hundred pieces appearing in media outlets and blogs around the world.

Coke didn't dare squash the story. In fact, it sent out a company-wide email with links to the radio show and other coverage, extolling the exposure. It posted *This American Life*'s piece on its Facebook page. One of the masters of consumer marketing seized the opportunity to talk about its secret recipe and how it was safely locked in a bank vault in Atlanta.

Classic Coke.

Chuck Salter is the son of the author and a senior writer for Fast Company, *a monthly business magazine.*

Herbs for What Ails You

ETON—Icy Plemons, the herb lady of Murray County, offered me a cup of tea, a brand that you won't find in a grocery store. Before taking a sip, I forgot my manners and asked what this tea contained. Mrs. Glenn Plemons, sixty-six, smiled and said, "This has twelve kinds of herbs, and I put honey in it. It will cure you of whatever ails you."

Actually, I wasn't ailing at that moment, and frankly I tried not to think about all of those roots and pieces of bark that had been boiled. My nose and taste buds couldn't deny the sort of earthy flavor of roots. I guess this unusual flavor has to grow on you.

She said this tea and a rub-on lotion made from five herbs provide relief from the pain and misery of arthritis. "Yes, I had arthritis so bad I couldn't bend my fingers," she said. "Now I can do anything I want to."

Mrs. Plemons, who identifies herself as an herbalist, is a native of Tennessee and a University of Georgia graduate who taught school for thirty-eight years.

She operates a beauty shop part time in her two-story, white frame house near Eton, about seven miles north of Chatsworth, but devotes most of her work hours to the collection and mixture of herbs that she sells for the treatment of numerous illnesses.

I wondered how she was given the unusual first name of Icy. "When I was born, my older sister came in, and she had a piece of ice on Valentine's Day, and she said, 'Mother, call her Icy,'" said Mrs. Plemons. "And they called me Icy."

Icy Plemons slices bark from a tree and adds it to her recipe for an herbal tea at her Murray County home. Many people ask the retired schoolteacher about the benefits of using herbs to treat skin cancer and arthritis.

Her interest in herbs dates back to her early childhood in Tennessee, where her father, James A. O'Neal, grew ginseng and several other plants for medicinal purposes. At the age of twelve, she was taught by her grandfather, John Houston O'Neal, how to mix three herbs to make a salve for treatment of skin cancer, she said. His brother, Robert, had learned the formula from an Indian in Oklahoma who told of its success in curing a cancer on his nose, Mrs. Plemons said. John was to try the same salve later when he, too, developed such a condition on his nose. Mrs. Plemons believes that more than three hundred skin cancers have been cured by the salve. She declined to reveal the ingredients.

She emphasized that when people visit her home to inquire about herb mixtures for treatment of diseases, she never diagnoses an illness, treats it herself or promises a cure. Instead, she explains that the herb mixtures have been effective in curing her own ailments or those of other persons who reported back to her of success.

More people inquire about the use of herbs to treat skin cancer and arthritis than any other disease.

She believes that a person with an internal cancer can be aided by chewing the bark of a slippery elm and drinking tea made from yellow root.

She and her husband search for herbs growing on sides of nearby mountains, and she orders numerous others from an out-of-state herb company. She showed me a package of white, powdered vitamin E that costs $60.40 per pound. Mrs. Plemons said she buys golden seal for $21.00 a pound.

She believes that constipation causes sinus trouble and arthritis. "That's what my mother and grandfather thought," she said. "They said people who were not constipated never had sinus or arthritis."

Her mother taught her to boil persimmon roots for treatment of colds, and her grandfather mixed herbs to make a medicine to combat diphtheria.

Does she have some means of treating acne that is so common among teenagers? "I've got a cure for it," said Mrs. Plemons, explaining her grandchild's "face cleared right up" and she ordered more herbs for another grandchild to use.

Mrs. Plemons said she learned how to brew a tea that a man could drink each day for sexual rejuvenation, although she explained later in a telephone interview that she isn't pushing sale of it. She likened the process to putting "a new motor in an old car" and indicated it might be best to "let younger folks" have their day.

The retired teacher believes that sexual impotency often is a mental rather than physical problem. She suggested possible help from a diet of eggs, vegetables, some slippery elm bark, yellow root tea and vitamin E. But stay away from the meats and sweets. Seafood, such as oysters, might be beneficial, she said.

Conscious of my own "high forehead," I asked what would cure baldness. "Get you a small box of pure lard, hog's lard," said Mrs. Plemons. "Mix it with red pepper (grown in a garden), let it get real hot in the stove and cook it a long time. Put it in a pint jar and use it to massage your scalp." She recalled the case of a Cleveland, Tennessee man who grew two inches of hair within six months after such a massage on a bald area of his head.

Mrs. Plemons believes that myrrh and golden seal will cure hay fever. "We make a tea," she said. "Pour a little in your hand, sniff it up your nose and drink three cups a day. It will take care of it."

She favors persimmon root tea for the flu and peach tree tea for an upset stomach.

What would give a woman's hair the sheen that is so desired? "You want an herb?" she asked. "I have it in the beauty shop. I also use willow bark. Make a tea and rinse your hair real good, and let it stay on for ten minutes."

Parked in her backyard is a black Cadillac that she bought "just for fun to say I did it with my herbs."

Mysterious Night of the Mull

WHITLOCK—The unusual experience will be remembered as the night of the mull. It began sort of like the opening chapter in a paperback spy novel that is sold in the corner drugstore.

One evening I walked into my house in Atlanta, and my wife said a man we didn't know had left his number for me to call. He was a ham radio operator who was asked by my Madison fishing buddy, Charles Cunningham, to request that I telephone him as soon as convenient.

Moments later I dialed Cunningham's home, and he said, "Bill Davis wants you to come to the mull."

The average Georgia housewife probably wouldn't go for that one. She would suspect that "mull" was a code name for a game of poker with the good ol' boys, a late appointment with the secretary or a night on the town without the spouse.

My "new, revised, expanded" $1.25 paperback dictionary was of little help. Take your choice: mull can mean "to grind, to ponder, to heat, sweeten."

I wondered if the British intelligence chief in *A Man Called Intrepid* ever assigned a beautiful brunette with the code name "Mull" to a World War II mission in France or Poland.

At six o'clock on the evening of the mull, I met Cunningham at his Madison home for the briefing. Then he and two piscatorial colleagues, "Foots" Gibbons and Lowery Hunt, rode with me to the remote Morgan County site. The unoccupied house on Davis's farm is what city folks call an antique. I was sorry that a windstorm last year knocked down the historic marker that read "Hernando DeSoto Slept Here."

Bill Davis (left) checks the flavor of a meat stew that he called a mull, while author Charles Salter stirs it with an old oak limb. This delicious stew contains venison, chicken, pork, turtle, onions, crackers, milk and secret seasoning. Occasionally, squirrels and rabbits are also put in the pot.

When we arrived, Bill Ponder waved his long arms and directed me to drive through the gate and park in a corner of the pasture. Ponder missed his calling. With such grace and form, he would have been a splendid Atlanta traffic cop.

The good ol' boys—my kind of folks, as we used to say in Waycross—were assembled under the tin roof of a shed, headquarters of the mull. The mysterious event turned out to be a magnificent country-style feast. Davis, the host, explained that a mull was a stew, and he introduced me to the chief cook, Bobby Youngblood, who, like Davis, is sworn to secrecy regarding the recipe.

The mull was simmering for its sixth or seventh hour in a ten-gallon black iron pot, the kind my ancestors used to do the week's wash in the Carolinas. All of us took turns stirring the mull with a long, antique board that once was part of a limb on an oak tree that offered the Spanish explorer, DeSoto, some shade and relief from the Georgia summer sun.

"I know the trade secrets of the mull," Davis said, "but we can't let it out. I can tell you it's got some venison, chicken, pork, turtle, onions, crackers and milk. And it has some secret seasoning and plenty of pepper. Sometimes we put squirrels and rabbit in the mull. Never a 'possum."

Harold "Cornbread" Cape, his partner in the timber business, pointed out that this same crowd gathers on a winter night for a "highway supper."

He tried to convince me that the wintertime mull is made with wildlife that didn't quite make it across highways. Usually six men can cover the county's roads in search of the animals between sundown and midnight.

Davis and Cornbread showed me the fifty-five-gallon drum with a hinged door and the barbecued venison on a rack over hot coals. Sometimes they barbecue goat in this manner.

"Men in Morgan County encourage women to eat barbecued goat because it gives them a good figure and makes them feel romantic," Davis explained. "Mull is very good for you, too. Mull eaters live longer, and it perks you up."

I found the mull and barbecued venison very delicious and filling, and the hot seasoning made me perspire almost enough to lose weight. What a delightful way to reduce.

Chief Vann's House

Spring Place—The handsome, three-story, federal-style house, standing on a hill overlooking the crossroads at Spring Place, was built in 1804 by a man "feared by many and loved by few." James Vann, son of an eighteenth-century Scotch trader and a Cherokee woman, was an Indian leader and wealthy plantation owner in what now is Murray County. Eager to see his people educated here deep in the Cherokee Nation, Vann helped the Moravian Brethren from North Carolina establish a mission and school at Spring Place in 1801. Moravian carpenters were among the skilled craftsmen who built the showplace of brick and heart pine.

A generous man when sober, Vann was known for acts of cruelty and violence when he became drunk on rum and whiskey.

Vann was only forty-one when he was shot to death in 1809 in Buffington's Tavern. A wooden marker on his grave in Forsyth County bore this epitaph: "Here lies the body of James Vann, who killed many a white man, and at last by a rifle volley fell, and the devil dragged his soul to hell."

In diaries at the Spring Place Mission, the Moravians were more charitable, writing, "Thus ended the life of one who was feared by many and loved by few in the 41st year of his life…Vann had been an instrument in the hand of God for establishing our mission in this nation. Never in his wildest orgies had he attempted to harm us. We could not but commend his soul to God's mercy."

Occupied by many different families until the mid-1940s, the house was in shambles—the roof and some flooring had collapsed and vandals had smashed all windows—when local citizens bought it and a three-acre tract in

Moravian carpenters and other craftsmen built this three-story, federal-style house in Spring Place, Georgia, in 1804 for James Vann, an Indian leader and plantation owner who was only forty-one when he was shot to death in a tavern. Moravian diaries said Vann "was feared by many and loved by few."

1952. They presented the property to the Georgia Historical Commission, which restored the house and furnished it with the aid of the Whitfield-Murray County Historical Society. The Vann house was dedicated in 1958 in ceremonies attended by forty-two of the descendants from Oklahoma.

Today, the house in Spring Place, three miles west of Chatsworth, is open to the public except on Mondays and is administered by the Parks, Recreation and Historic Sites Division of the Georgia Department of Natural Resources. James Hall is the superintendent, and his wife, Pat, is the interpretive ranger.

On the front and back of the house, four pairs of white pilasters rise two stories, capped by a classic cornice, with fan lighted doors on each porch and balcony. The first floor has a large hall, a very rare "hanging" or "floating" staircase, a twenty- by thirty-foot drawing room and a dining room of the same dimensions. The kitchen was in a separate building behind the house as a fire safety measure.

Walter Smith of Augusta, who travels widely doing construction and maintenance work for the state parks and historic sites division, said he still hasn't figured out how the stairs were made. The stairs, with beautiful carvings including Cherokee roses on the undersides of platforms, appear to be hanging or floating, with absolutely no visible means of support. A state pamphlet calls the stairway "the oldest example of cantilevered construction in Georgia." A true cantilever is a bracket, block or beam anchored in a wall to provide support for a stairway or balcony.

Chief Vann and the Moravian carpenters performed quite a trick of magic, I guess, making invisible cantilevers. Mrs. Hall said a number of architects touring the house over the years also have found the stairs quite baffling in design. "I can build hanging stairs but would have to extend it out on the other side for something to hang from," Smith said. "Something has to extend to hold it."

A few years after the house was restored by the state, workers installed a steel rod to hold the floating stairway. I guess someone's faith was about to run out.

A visitor notes that Vann built Christian doors featuring the cross and an open Bible. When opened, the doors rise a bit above the floor so that they close without help of a human hand.

Hanging over a large fireplace in the dining room is a painting of Vann's son, Joseph, known as Rich Joe Vann, who lived here until the Georgia militia forced him out in 1834 after the land lotteries began in the Cherokee Nation. On the second floor are two large bedrooms, each measuring twenty by thirty feet, and another large hall. The third floor contains two coffin-shaped rooms, which also were likely used as bedrooms by Vann or his son's family.

Cherokee roses are prominently featured on the arched and columned overmantels. An interior decorator scraped through nearly twenty layers of paint, revealing that Chief Vann had been inspired by the beauty of nature in selecting the color schemes. Colors on the parlor's big overmantel reminded Vann of the red clay, green trees and grass, blue sky and yellow, ripe grain and also wildflowers.

Mrs. Hall said visitors to the house are especially curious about the dungeon with an earthen floor in which Vann confined some of his estimated two hundred black slaves when they were disobedient or disorderly.

She showed me a charred mark left on the house's stairway the day in 1834 that Georgia troops came to evict Vann's son, Joseph, and his family. Joseph Vann had hired a white man as his plantation overseer, not realizing he violated a new state law prohibiting an Indian from employing a white person. At that time, white settlers also were receiving land grants of 160 acres each in a lottery system in the Cherokee territory.

When the Georgia militia arrived at Vann's house, a white boarder, Spencer Riley, tried to claim the property and was wounded in a gun battle on the stairs. Colonel William Bishop placed a piece of burning wood on the stairs, and thinking the house was on fire, Riley fled.

Joseph Vann took his family to his other farm in Tennessee, built a racetrack and added to his fortune. Later, the family moved to Oklahoma, where thousands of Cherokees had resettled.

A steamboat business venture ultimately led to his untimely death in 1844. Vann and guests aboard his steamboat, the *Lu Walker*, were killed when the boiler exploded during a race on the Ohio River near Louisville.

Shortly before his death, the federal government finally paid Vann $19,605 for his North Georgia property. The holdings had included the plantation house, eight hundred acres under cultivation, forty-two cabins, six barns, a sawmill, a gristmill, five smokehouses, a blacksmith shop and foundry, a trading post, a peach kiln, a whiskey still, 1,133 peach trees and 147 apple trees.

Mr. Bass Tells Turtle Tales

FACEVILLE—The night air was hot and sticky as threatening clouds parked in the sky over Lake Seminole, warning critters in water and woods of an approaching storm in southwest Georgia. Several women talked and laughed in a butterbean-shelling party on the café porch at Jack Wingate's fishing camp. The menfolk were discussing the appetites and unpredictable behavior of wary old largemouth bass.

A balding, stout man with a gruff voice could promise his friends there'd be a shower soon. His knee was aching, and he anchored himself in a wooden chair, dreading the painful steps back to his pickup camper for the ride home to Chipley, Florida, sixty-five miles south.

Uley Bass, sixty-three, tells turtle rather than bass tales, but the shelled devils have big mouths, too. For fifteen years he has been setting out short trotlines and bush lines and baiting hooks with meat to catch loggerhead and soft shell turtles, which he sells alive—often in Louisiana—to folks who are fond of the delicious meat. He showed me several big turtle shells and skulls that a Florida friend polished. "You can line the inside with felt or other cloth and have a mighty pretty nut or fruit bowl for the table," said Bass's old buddy, Wingate.

Bass easily convinced me that turtle catching can be a risky venture. He held up his left hand, and I saw that two fingers were missing. "It happened late one night about twelve years ago," Bass said.

I think everybody on the café porch was about to break out in goose pimples.

"A seventy-five-pound loggerhead turtle did it," he said. "It was all my fault. My son and I had caught him while 'gator huntin'. We were in shallow

Uley Bass (left) and Jack Wingate hold shells of big turtles that were caught in Lake Seminole. Bass, observing that it can be a dangerous venture, lost two fingers when a seventy-five-pound loggerhead turtle chomped down on his hand.

water, and when he surfaced, I grabbed his tail and brought him in the boat. I was astraddle the turtle's shell on the middle seat with his tail toward the bow and his head behind me. My boy was on the back seat. I'd laid my paddle down."

A moment after they spotted an alligator, the small outboard motor's propeller became tangled in moss. "I was tryin' to hold my light on the 'gator and reached for the paddle to help my boy get out of the moss bed. I reached back, and the turtle got my fingers. I didn't know it was done. I thought it mashed it a little bit. It didn't hurt one bit."

He continued, "My boy said, 'Daddy, didn't that thing bite your fingers off?' I said, 'No, it just mashed 'em a bit.' And he said, 'Daddy, I saw something fly off in the boat.'"

Bass touched his left hand, felt two nubs and saw blood gushing out, and he knew he was in trouble.

You could have heard a butterbean hit the ground as Bass added, "The blood sealed off pretty quick. We went up the hill and loaded the boat on the trailer and got to my house, twenty-five miles from there, and I was as sick as a mule. I got me a Coca-Cola, and it settled my stomach."

Bass became interested in catching turtles sort of by accident one night years ago when he and a Louisiana friend were hunting alligators. They had left baited hooks six to eight inches above the surface, but a very heavy rain raised the creek's level and covered the pieces of meat in muddy water. "We went up and checked the lines and pulled out a big turtle," Bass said. "We shot him in the head with a .22 Hornet and got three turtles that night, all big'uns."

He was surprised when his friend promised he'd send his share of the money he got for the fifty-pound turtles. "He sent me a check for forty-nine dollars, and I looked at it and thought, that's all right," Bass said. "So, I got started bush-hookin' for turtles. I learned right quick where to put it. Don't go to a straight bank 'cause he's got a hole up under there, and he'll go under and get your hook lost. I found you go to a sandbar-type bank and they'll come up on it and you can get 'em."

Bass, frankly, is glad Florida outlawed baskets for catching turtles. "It takes a smart man to fool with baskets and save turtles," he said. "If he's a sleepy head, the turtles get in the basket and drown and the meat spoils. Sometimes they leave 'em, too. Baskets ought to be ruled out."

A Florida angler told him that fishing in a slough is much better after turtles are removed. During the spawning season of gamefish and panfish, turtles try to raid the nests to devour eggs.

The biggest loggerhead turtle that Bass ever caught was a 116-pounder that he delivered in Louisiana.

"We catch them from around March 15 until October 15 when the water is warm," Bass said. "If the moon is all-night light, I don't even try it. It's good for soft shells, though. You can put out lines late in the evenin'. If the moon is rising two hours after dark, what turtles you catch will be on the lines then. Now, if the moon is setting at three o'clock in the morning, you'd just as well go home and get in the bed because they'll get on the lines just before daylight."

I would much rather saw logs in a soft bed than risk my fingers reaching for turtles on bush lines in a lake or creek at night.

Teacher Loves Country Music

MADISON—A sixty-one-year-old Morgan County school teacher has loved country music ever since he was a youngster helping his father plow with a mule on a farm near Statesboro.

Many rural Georgians are fond of country and hillbilly music, so Leo Hall's taste in songs wouldn't seem out of the ordinary.

But Leo Hall is black.

He smiles and says he vividly remembers that in his youth, it was exceedingly rare to find a black person in Georgia who liked his kind of music. Most black people in the 1920s and 1930s preferred spirituals and popular songs, and some made history singing and playing jazz or the blues. Later they were to sing and dance to rhythm and blues and rock and roll.

Hall says he is happy to see an increasing number of blacks interested in country music, perhaps due to the popularity of a fine singer named Charlie Pride.

Hall was thrilled to hear students loudly applaud when he sang country songs while the principal played the guitar at Morgan County High, where he is a vocational agriculture and horticulture teacher.

"When I was going to high school, my friends kidded me for liking country music," Hall said. "I sang and played a guitar and did some yodeling, but they didn't like it." One of his school pals observed, "That's white folks' music."

But Hall disagreed, explaining it was everybody's music.

Agriculture teacher Leo Hall checks some of his plants in the school's greenhouse. When he was in high school, his friends did not understand why he liked country music, sang, played a guitar and even did some yodeling.

He graduated from the school that later became Savannah State College and studied one year at Ohio State. For twenty-seven years he has been a teacher.

"When I was only eight or nine years old, I wanted a guitar, but my daddy was not able to buy one," Hall said. "I got me an old cigar box, put a staff on it and used a screen wire for strings, and could make pretty good tunes with it. I was twelve or thirteen when I worked in tobacco fields for fifty cents a day and saved enough to buy an old guitar for seven dollars from a neighbor."

As a soldier for three years in the army in World War II, he occasionally sang country songs in the barracks at night, but his black friends couldn't understand why he liked the music.

Hall saw a dream come true when he cut an eight-track tape of some popular country selections, backed by Bill Ashley's band from Madison. Among the songs are such favorites as "I'd Rather Love You," "There Goes My Everything" and "Kiss an Angel Good Morning."

This summer he plans to record another tape, and he soon will be the guest performer in an Athens club. "If I were twenty-one years old again," Hall said, "oh, man, I'd go full blast for a country music singing career."

Hall's exposure as a singer had been limited to appearances at churches or the high school's stage until he received an invitation to appear in the annual follies at the Madison-Morgan County Cultural Center two years ago. He was a very proud man when he received a big ovation from the packed auditorium for his renditions of "Mona Lisa" and "Back Home Again." Hall was flattered when local bandleader Bill Ashley invited him "to go over some songs," and a few weeks later, he was called to sing at another show.

"I just like to sing country music," Hall said. "Country music, to me, explains a lot of things. It tells a story, some happy ones, some sad ones. Rock music doesn't tell you much."

He said some songs appeal to him because they stir memories of his youth on a Georgia farm. "I like songs that related to something centered around the farm and country," he said. "I loved the farm and loved farm life and the outdoors. Many days I held in my hand the soil that grew the crops, and I plowed fields with a mule, so I have deep feelings about the country."

Years later, he found it satisfying to teach agriculture in the classroom and then take students to the school's greenhouse, where they learned how to grow vegetables and ornamental plants.

Hall says he regrets that pop and rock have influenced some of the sounds coming out of Nashville today. "They have taken some of the country songs and tried to soup them up," he said with a smile. "They're getting a little bit away from true country. I like the straight, down-to-earth country songs."

His favorite singers include Charlie Pride, Eddie Arnold, Elvis Presley, Jim Reeves, Dolly Parton and Loretta Lynn. "Loretta Lynn sings from the heart and does a great job," he said.

Hall said it would be only fitting that a good country song be sung before he is laid to rest. "Should I die tomorrow, I would like to have somebody sing 'I'd Rather Love You' at my funeral."

I wonder if St. Peter ever strums a guitar at the Golden Gate to welcome the new arrivals?

Teller of Tall Swamp Tales

FARGO—One of the heroes of my youth was a tall, slender, barefoot man in overalls, the most colorful character ever to leave footprints on the banks of the Suwannee River. Everybody simply called him Lem.

Elemuel L. Griffis operated a fishing camp on the edge of the Okefenokee Swamp, twelve miles northeast of Fargo on what now is Georgia Route 177. His widow, Alice, still runs the fishing camp on a tract of land on which Lem's great-grandfather grew corn before the Civil War.

For forty years Lem took sightseers and fishermen on the Suwannee River and deep into the "land of trembling earth," and he probably was more knowledgeable about the Okefenokee's game and fish than anybody on Earth.

Lem, who died at the age of seventy-two in 1968, is remembered fondly by thousands of folks as the teller of the "tallest of tall yarns."

He only attended school three years, dropping out to work on his father's farm and then for a timber company as a young man. About 1925, he began taking parties into the swamp for about fifty cents a day. Lem told a friend that he "learned to write in the sand." He did a considerable amount of reading over the years and was recognized as being a shrewd businessman.

He was very proud of his two sons and two daughters when they attended college in Douglas and Valdosta.

Lem used to boil coffee in a big bucket over an open fire and fry fish at a wooden cook shelter on Big Water, a swamp lake. He would tell the fishermen, "This coffee is as black as Jack Johnson, strong as Gene Tunney [both famed heavyweight boxers] and as hot as the place the preacher talks about."

Lem Griffis, a fishing camp owner and guide, shows a visitor to the Okefenokee Swamp the Billy's Island site of an Indian village that was found by army General Charles R. Floyd on November 11, 1838. Griffis told tall yarns and guided fishermen and sightseers on the Suwannee River and in the swamp. *Courtesy of Edwin A. Griffis.*

The beloved swamper enjoyed telling folks, "The Okefenokee is so boggy you can stir it with a stick and bubbles will go down, and it's so thick you have to back up to bat your eyes."

His son, Edwin Alphin Griffis, principal of Fargo Elementary School, chuckled in recalling a prank often pulled on visitors camping in the swamp. "My father said that if they felt a snake, they shouldn't move or it might bite them," he said. "In those days the outboard motors had crank ropes. After the fishermen had gone to sleep, my father would take the cold, damp crank rope, dip in the water and drag it across someone's neck. It felt like a snake, and the man jumped up scared."

Many years ago, a rather intoxicated fisherman began teasing a bear cub chained to a stake at the camp. "He was sitting on the ground, and he turned to speak to friends, and the bear swatted him on the head and flattened his hat," Alphin said. The man told Lem he wanted to buy the bear, explaining, "I think I have found something that will whip my wife."

On a hot summer day, Lem told a fishing party, "Be careful or you'll get bear-caught." This was translated to mean a person might be overcome by the intense heat.

In a small book entitled *The Tallest of Tall Yarns*, published in 1944, Lem wrote, "One day while out fishing, a large bass came up to get my plug [artificial lure]. When he opened his mouth to get the plug, the water in the lake all ran in. If he had not of closed his mouth and spit the water out, I would of had to left the boat and walked back."

He liked to tell a fisherman that he sold trained minnows, and when the fish bites, he shouldn't jerk his pole to set the hook. "When the fish tries to swallow him, he runs through his gills. So when you get a bite, you don't want to jerk. You just count the bites you get until you get all on the line you want, then pull them out and go on. You don't even have to wait to string them."

Many visitors to the swamp were very fearful of the big alligators and suspected deadly snakes might fall from overhanging limbs into the boat. Lem enjoyed informing the city folks, "Luckily we have never had anyone drowned in any of the lakes in the Okefenokee. If a person falls overboard, an alligator always swallows them before they have time to be drowned."

He also told tall yarns about the weather in the Okefenokee. "The wet weather has caused me to lose lots of my hogs. Mud got to collecting on their tails and drying into a hard ball. Finally that ball got so large and heavy it stretched the skin so tight the hogs could not bat their eyes, and the poor things died from want of sleep."

Lem told fishermen the Okefenokee was a very healthful place to reside. "We have not had but one death in the past ten years," he said. "That was a doctor. He starved to death. We had to kill a man to start a graveyard."

His wife was the subject of some good-natured humor. "I don't know much about these ladies' clubs," Lem said. "All I know is my wife has a large one and is an expert in using it."

"I never get to drive my car anymore. All I do is set under the steering wheel. My wife does all the driving. When I come in late for supper, my wife makes it hot for me—hot tongue and cold shoulder."

Family Life in Okefenokee

FARGO—Visitors to Griffis Fishing Camp on the Suwannee River sometimes stop and stare intently at what they believe is a primitive canoe cut out of a cypress tree. Alice Griffis smiles and explains, "This was the first washing machine in the Okefenokee Swamp."

Tourists invariably do a double-take and suspect she's got to be kidding. "It's funny," said the sixty-six-year-old Mrs. Griffis. "Visitors can't understand it. Soap and water were put in this cut-out section to wash clothes. And I've still got the batting stick that was used to hit the clothes when they were laid here on the end."

She has lived here since 1929, when she moved to a farm close to the Suwannee's banks as the teenage bride of Lem Griffis, who was to gain fame as a fishing camp operator and humorist who told mighty tall tales. Since his death in 1968 at the age of seventy-two, she has continued to operate the fishing camp, located on Georgia 177 about twelve miles northeast of tiny Fargo.

Their two sons and two daughters used to travel eighty miles round trip by bus daily to attend a Homerville high school, and all four attended college in Douglas and Valdosta.

"I was a country girl from Homerville and hadn't been in the swamp before," said Mrs. Griffis. "I thought it was beautiful. I don't get to go in there much anymore. Not much time to take off now."

In those days, the Griffises had a number of farming neighbors and friends, including the Lee family that still lived on nearby Billy's Island in the Okefenokee. "They used to hunt alligators in the summer and fur-bearing

Cypress trees and Spanish moss are reflected on the surface of Billy's Lake in the Okefenokee Swamp, Georgia's "land of the trembling earth." Lem and Alice Griffis raised two sons and two daughters in their home near the Suwannee River.

animals in the winter," she said. "We had the fishing camp and a restaurant. I cooked for my family and the fishermen, and my day started around four-thirty or five o'clock."

Mrs. Griffis rode by car or truck to Fargo or Homerville on a dirt road to buy supplies such as coffee, sugar, one-hundred-pound bags of cornmeal, forty-eight-pound bags of flour and whole sides of white bacon. "Part of the time you got stuck in the mud, and part of the time you were stuck in the sand, according to what the weather conditions were," she said, smiling.

The family owned hogs and cows that roamed freely in the forest. Sometimes a black bear would catch a slow cow for dinner, and Lem once lost a fine hunting dog to a hungry alligator.

"All of my children were born at home," she said. "I had a big clothesline, an outside clothes drier, not an electric one. Clothes in the sunshine and fresh air smelled so good. Along then, we were known as a better-off family. It was in the Depression. We grew a lot of our food and had plenty of fish to eat and pork and beef."

The Griffis family was quite progressive and enjoyed some firsts for that community. "In the 1930s Lem had a Delco generator, and we had electricity before the others," she said. "We had the first radio around here, and people from Fargo came out to hear the radio. Years later we were the first to have a television set and the only ones who got good reception. They'd drive down here from Fargo to eat supper with us and watch the boxing on TV." Electric power lines did not reach many of the rural homes until the 1940s.

Home remedies frequently were used to treat illnesses that struck family members whose houses were on unpaved roads miles from a doctor's office. Mrs. Griffis said Lem's mother, Mrs. Elizabeth Mixon Griffis, was "an old-fashioned doctor in this part of the country." She recalled, "They came to get her all times of the day or night for the old remedies. She doctored people with herbs and made tea, and they'd get better. She drank sassafras tea for high blood pressure. A boy had whooping cough. She made an onion poultice."

Her four children's friends from Fargo and Homerville used to enjoy visiting the fishing camp, especially in the summer, and nearly every day the house "was filled with teenagers." The kids liked to go swimming in the Suwannee River, paddle canoes and johnboats on sightseeing excursions and fish in the Okefenokee's many lakes. "They were never bored," she said. "I never had any problems with any of my children."

Living in such a remote area, how did she motivate her children to study and continue pushing back their horizons? Mrs. Griffis laughed and said, "Well, I used to tell them when they sat down to do homework, 'All right, get busy with your books. You don't want to grow up and be dumb like your mother.' And they'd look at me and laugh and come back with some kind of funny saying. Sometimes one would ask me about birds, and I'd say, 'I never had time to study birds. No, I had to work.'"

In a few minutes of conversation with Mrs. Griffis, a visitor knows she is indeed quite an intelligent lady, and he admires her for the superb job she performed raising four children.

Mrs. Griffis said many tourists sincerely believe "there are still Indians and wild people" living in the Okefenokee. "I'll be talking to a tourist, and he will say, 'Are the wild people out there in the swamp?' and I'll say, 'I'm one of them.' They really believe the swamp has wild people who would run from them and hide behind the bushes," she said.

Country Cooking Fit for a President

FARGO—It's a tummy-growling shame that Alice Griffis doesn't operate a restaurant anymore at her fishing camp on the Suwannee River. For forty years or more, she served some of the finest old-fashioned country cooking that could be tasted south of the Mason-Dixon line.

Her husband, Lem, who died in 1968 at the age of seventy-two, had guided parties of fishermen and sightseers on the river and deep into the Okefenokee Swamp since the late 1920s. Most of them went home bragging about their big catches of gamefish and panfish. I suspect 100 percent of them were also praising the delicious country food that Mrs. Griffis, sixty-six, put on the tables three times a day.

One of the folks who especially enjoyed his meals at the fishing camp was a young peanut farmer named Jimmy Carter of Plains, Georgia. He was a friend of Lem and Alice over the years, and as governor, he visited the camp for some relaxing fishing.

Mrs. Griffis remembers that he broke into a big smile that later was to become familiar to the whole nation and said, "That was the best food I ever have eaten." She modestly replied, "No, it was not. You were just hungry after being in the swamp all day." He again praised her cooking, and he didn't forget the gentle, hardworking woman who raised two sons and two daughters, all of whom attended college.

Mrs. Griffis received an invitation to attend his inauguration as president of the United States. She might have been the only resident of the Okefenokee to be so honored. She teased a neighbor and said maybe she would become

Alice Griffis holds a nearly eleven-foot-long collard stalk at the fishing camp that her husband, Lem, operated on the Suwannee River in the Okefenokee Swamp. Her restaurant was known for its delicious southern country dishes. A fan of her cooking was a peanut farmer and future president, Jimmy Carter.

the White House cook. But she was unable to leave her business to attend the historic event.

I grew hungry imagining the feast that fishermen were served in her restaurant. The menu included country ham, gravy, sausage, eggs, grits, big biscuits, honey and syrup and coffee. I remember that after frying ham and removing it, my mother would pour coffee into the skillet containing ham grease and heat it to make red-eye gravy, which was delicious on grits and biscuits.

Dinners and suppers featured fresh vegetables, pork, beef and fish that were caught in the Suwannee River or the Okefenokee Swamp. "In the summer, we had field peas, beans, okra, corn and other vegetables. We grew some of them," she said. "And I cooked pone corn bread. You boil bacon or ham and cook collard greens and bake sweet potatoes. That's what they call good eating."

In the autumn and early winter, the Griffis family grew turnips, collards and mustard, and they cured sausage and hams in the smokehouse. "We used to have lots of cattle, and Lem would kill one, butcher it out, salt it down, cut it up and let it lie in the salt a few days," she said. "Then he would hang it up and smoke it with oak fire smoke. You could slice that up when you wanted it and cook grits, eggs and red-eye gravy and sometimes rice."

A few years ago when oil riggers were working nearby, Mrs. Griffis was asked to cook some wild game that didn't stimulate her appetite. "We had a big corn crop, and those men wanted to kill some 'coons for me to cook," she said. "One man killed four at a time. He dressed them, put them in water and hung them up to dry. After I got through with cooking breakfast, I would boil them and put onions in the pan and bake them. The 'coons smelled so good cooking. I never did taste the 'coons, though. Just the thought of it, I couldn't."

Some of the fishermen were attracted by the aroma of the raccoons, but when she identified the meat, they usually lost interest.

"Once I cooked some 'gator tail for the crew hands," Mrs. Griffis said. "They brought two dish pans full of that meat. No, I didn't taste that either. I got so sick of smelling it. After they ate dinner, I took the rest of the meat out and buried it. I used to cook turtle a lot, too."

She added, "The last thing they brought me to cook was a big old rattlesnake. I wouldn't cook it. No rattlesnake cooking for me. I told them to go to Fargo and buy a frying pan."

Memories of a Barefoot Boy

OCILLA—A skinny, blond, barefoot boy wearing a tee-shirt and short pants used to run and play in the shade of big oak trees on the grounds of the Irwin County Courthouse. Surely those trees were the tallest in the whole wide world, the boy thought.

As dinnertime approached on a summer day, he would glance up at the courthouse clock and hope his mother was frying a chicken. Sometimes he wished that he could turn into a squirrel for just one day so he could climb the oaks, jump from limb to limb and throw acorns at the humans on the ground.

Today that boy is a six-foot man who has lost half his blond hair, gained more inches at the waistline than he wants and moved to a city where many folks never take time to watch squirrels play. I drove past that old courthouse for the first time in many years and regretted to note the clock isn't running anymore. A county official says he doesn't think those hands have moved around the big clock's face in more than ten years.

This spring and summer, the folks in Ocilla will be walking in more sunshine than ever on the courthouse grounds. A number of the giant oaks, very old and sick, had to be chopped down less than a month ago.

The first seven years of my life were spent in Ocilla, where my father, the late J.D. Salter, was a schoolteacher, basketball coach and principal in the 1930s. An old family friend, Newton Hancock, showed me the two-story wooden house where my parents rented an apartment until we moved from Ocilla to Greensboro in the summer of 1940.

Author Charles Salter as a child in a cowboy suit in Ocilla, Georgia, where he spent the first seven years of his life. He enjoyed seeing Tarzan and western movies at the local "picture show," where a ticket, soft drink and popcorn cost only a few nickels and dimes.

The sight of those front steps brought back the painful memory of my first traffic accident. My tricycle and I took a tumble to the bottom, but my teeth and bones somehow didn't break.

A big tree in the backyard must be the same one I climbed to tie a rope on a limb for a swing like the one Tarzan used in the Saturday movie. The "lord of the jungle" was swinging on a vine because the stores that sold rope were beyond walking distance.

The old theater—we called it the picture show—where kids flocked on Saturdays with nickels and dimes to see Tarzan and western movies and "continued serials" now is used as a small-loan office. Each week, the action-packed serials left us hanging in suspense wondering if the hero survived, and we returned the next Saturday to see what happened.

I wonder if kids in small towns today consider a trip to the dime store sort of exciting. Of course, you can't find a toy for a dime. To get a Coke with a pretzel hanging on the side of the glass at the drugstore was quite a treat.

Passing the barbershop, I remembered waiting my turn to crawl onto the huge, padded chair for a haircut that cost less than a dollar. It was here that men had sweet-smelling stuff rubbed onto their heads or faces. A little boy didn't want that mess on him because his buddies would call him a sissy. In those days, of course, only women went to the beauty parlors.

Standing in front of the First Baptist Church, I chuckled in recalling how I once smuggled comic books into the sanctuary. In those days I think the air-conditioning system in every pew consisted of hand-held, thin, cardboard fans advertising a funeral home. I remember all of the ladies wore hats. So did most of the men. A woman got upset if she spotted someone wearing a hat like hers. At that stage of my life, I couldn't understand why it mattered.

Once Dad took me to a tobacco auction in nearby Tifton. He was then smoking Lucky Strike cigarettes, and I was amazed to discover that the big, golden leaves on the warehouse floor were going to fit someday into little cigarettes. In a large, hot warehouse, the tobacco auctioneer was chanting rapidly some words that I was sure nobody could understand. It would be fun to talk so fast and be paid money for playing this game, I thought. The idea of making tobacco burn and actually inhaling the smoke into one's lungs seemed to be a doggone dumb idea to me at that time.

Sense of Belonging Gone

ATHENS—I was mighty tempted to take off my shoes and climb the sweetgum trees on Morton Avenue again. But I came to my senses and realized that a forty-five-year-old man playing Tarzan might frighten the local residents and wind up in the state hospital in Milledgeville.

Memories flooded my mind as I walked down the street where I had lived in a duplex apartment during those carefree years from the third through the eighth grade. Morton Avenue still is quiet and shaded, but as I suspected, the trees are an awful lot bigger, and somehow the houses have become smaller. Nobody swings on a vine like Tarzan across a gully in the nearby woods anymore. Houses were built where some trees had stood in the early 1940s.

The plum bushes—I ate the plums at a green and sour stage—are gone, replaced by a brick house. A persimmon tree, the fruit of which turned my mouth inside out, would be in someone's living room if it had survived.

A number of college students rent houses or apartments on the street now, and the kids I knew have grown up and moved away.

Is there anybody left who puts on a swimsuit and runs with joy in the street during a summer shower? Does anyone still tie a string on a June bug's leg and catch honeybees in an empty mayonnaise jar?

I paused and looked at a small, brick house around the corner and remembered how fifth-grade boys and girls cried unashamed one day and wondered why their classmate, John, had to die. Until that day, some of us honestly thought that death came only to the old, wrinkled, gray-haired people. I vividly recall that some of the youngsters were puzzled when the

Charles Salter at about age twelve in Athens. Decades later, he returned to the Morton Avenue neighborhood, where his sense of belonging was gone forever, and he remembered that the third-grade class heard President Roosevelt's radio address after the Japanese bombed Pearl Harbor.

teacher wiped the tears from her own eyes and said solemnly, "It was God's will that he go home with Him."

Across Pine Crest Drive, I saw the former home of Charles McMillan and remembered injuring my right shin trying to jump like Captain Marvel onto the brick porch. I was told that a number of years ago, that old friend was killed in a traffic accident.

On Morton Avenue, I wondered if anyone plays days-long Monopoly games the way Charles Bell and I did one summer. He later joined President John F. Kennedy's Peace Corps and died of a heart attack in Colombia, South America.

Standing in the street, I remembered the thrill of seeing two B-17s roar at low altitude over the neighborhood one summer day in 1942 during World War II.

Several blocks up Pine Crest Drive, boys and girls in a third-grade classroom in Barrow Elementary School had gathered around a radio to hear President Franklin D. Roosevelt say that December 7, 1941, was "a day that will live in infamy." Many kids didn't know what infamy meant, but soon they would learn every verse of "Comin' in on a Wing and a Prayer,"

Side Trips

"Remember Pearl Harbor" and "White Cliffs of Dover." And every boy wished he could be a fighter pilot and shoot down a Japanese Zero.

Later, walking with a whistle in knickers—"whistle britches"—a boy would ask his buddies, "Have you seen that picture of Betty Grable's legs that all the pilots and sailors want?"

I was a blond, very skinny kid in those days, known as Cotton or Salty, and frequently rode my bicycle to the Georgia Bulldogs' afternoon football practice. In the 1941 season, the kids' hero was a flat-footed University of Georgia back named Frank Sinkwich, and in 1946 we thought Bulldogs halfback Charley Trippi was the greatest football player in the United States.

I laughed in glancing at another front yard and remembered how every boy on the street wished he could do cartwheels or walk on his hands as skillfully as Frances Wyatt and Betty McCants, the neighborhood's best acrobats.

At the top of the steep driveway at the former home of Marian Hinton, I remembered only one or two people had the courage to fly down it on roller skates.

In that backyard one day, I played Superman, with a towel around my neck for a cape, and chased two girls, who were the bandits. I ran into a clothesline that was mouth-high and lost a tooth before landing on my back just inches from a stob beside a rose bush. A few years later, I was to learn that grown men chased pretty women, too, with more romantic intentions.

Some of the youngsters in Athens today might be surprised to know that all the kids in my old neighborhood had to do chores, such as drying dishes, dusting and sweeping, before they could go out and play.

Sonny Lear, a grammar school pal down the street, suggested that we convert our cast-iron toy soldiers into British commandos. To darken them for a night attack, we simply left them a few minutes in his father's coal-burning furnace in the basement.

Alva Mayes, next door, now a Macon doctor, provided lumber for us to saw into shapes of machine guns for the neighborhood commando squad. He carved himself an army .45 pistol that all of us wanted but never got in a trade.

The Baptist preacher would have been horrified if he had known I was thumbing through a Big Little Book during a fire and brimstone sermon on Sunday mornings.

To this very day, I still wonder what a friend saw or heard a moment before leaping from the second-floor window of an empty, obviously haunted house on a Halloween night. He was bruised and scared and convinced us we'd be crazy to go into that house. We agreed, naturally.

It's a strange feeling to walk down a familiar street and know that you won't ever belong there again.

Index

A

Armour, Lucy Mae 66, 67, 68
Athens, GA 154, 167, 169
Atkinson, GA 51, 52
Atkinson, Teddy 33
Auraria, GA 35, 37, 84

B

Bartow, General F.S. 16
Bass, Uley 149, 150, 151
Battle at Gettysburg 15, 18
Beal, Everett 7, 133
Beal, Judy 133
Bell, Charles 168
Blairsville, GA 94
Brown, Governor Joe 92
Burnt Fort, GA 51

C

Calhoun, GA 61
Cannon, Oscar 63, 64, 65
Canton, GA 24
Capone, Al 69, 70, 71
Carson, Allan 25
Carson, Fiddlin' John 25, 26, 27, 28
Carter, President Jimmy 10, 43, 44,
    47, 161

Cartersville, GA 22, 89
Civil War 15, 80, 84, 91, 93, 117, 155
Clark, Roy 27
Cleveland, Cade 44, 47
Cleveland, GA 30
Cleveland, Windell 43, 44, 46
Cobb, General T.R.R. 17
Coca-Cola 9, 133, 134, 135, 137, 151
Collins, Floyd 26
Collis, Junior 77
Cork, GA 85
Cunningham, Charles 7, 142

D

Darien, GA 32, 34, 82, 83, 84
Davis, Bill 96, 142, 144
Davis, Jefferson 17, 92
Davis, Will 94, 96, 97
D-Day invasion 30
Deriso, Dr. Clark 112
Deriso, Melinda 112, 113, 114, 115
DeSoto, Hernando 77, 78, 142, 144
Donalsonville, GA 25, 28
Duluth, GA 75

E

Eatonton, GA 109, 110, 111
Elberton, GA 43, 44, 122, 124

Ellijay, GA 20
Elliott, Charlie 49
Elliott, Jack 49
Ellis, Jim 44
Eton, GA 139

F

Faceville, GA 149
Fargo, GA 155, 156, 158, 159, 160, 161, 163
Felker, Hester 15, 18
Fitzpatrick, Mary-Ann Perry 104, 105, 106, 107
Floyd, Duff 19, 20, 21, 22, 23
Frank, Leo 26

G

Gainesville 7, 9, 54, 56, 94, 133
Gale, Dave 32
Gale, Everett "Greek" 32, 33, 34
Gale, Frankie 32, 34
Gault, Clyde 33
Glades, GA 54
Glass, Ira 8, 11, 136, 137, 138
Greene, Nathanael 79
Greensboro 10, 116, 164, 175
Griffin, GA 7, 69, 133
Griffis, Alice 158, 159, 160, 161, 163
Griffis, Edwin Alphin 156
Griffis, Elemuel "Lem" 155, 158, 160, 163

H

Hall, Leo 152, 153, 154
Hancock, Newton 164
Hardin, John Henry 23
Harris, Roy 27
Hawes, Lilla 79, 80, 81
Hay, Agnes 85, 87, 88
Hay, Vivian 85, 87, 88
Heardmont, GA 122
Higgins, Ted 56, 57
Hill, Joshua 91, 92, 93, 126
Hinton, Marian 169

Howell, Hubert 22, 23, 24
Hunt, Caroline 91, 92

J

Jasper, GA 19
Johnson, Rosa Lee 25, 26, 27, 28
Jones, Grandpa 27

K

Kennedy, President John F. 10, 37, 104, 107, 108, 168
Kitchens, William "Prophet" 127, 128, 129

L

Laughing Gal 24
Lear, Sonny 169
Lee, General Robert E. 18
Lewis, Bessie 82, 84
Loyd, J.B. 48, 49, 50
Lynn, Loretta 27, 154

M

Madison, GA 7, 9, 66, 91, 92, 125, 126, 127, 142, 152, 153
Mayes, Alva 169
McCants, Betty 169
McCommons, Carlene 116, 117, 118, 119
McCommons, Roger "Deeta" 116, 118
McDaniel, Henry 15, 16, 17, 18
McDaniel, Ira 16
Meaders, Lanier 29, 30, 31
Monroe, GA 8, 15, 18
Moonshine Kate 25, 26
Mossy Creek 29

N

Nelson, Judd 60, 61, 62

O

Ocilla, GA 10, 63, 164, 175
Oglethorpe, General James 45, 81, 83

Okefenokee Swamp 155, 156, 157, 158, 160, 161, 163
Oswald, Lee Harvey 9, 104, 106, 107

P

Parks, Benjamin 36
Pemberton, John S. 134, 137
Phagan, Mary 26
Pine Log, GA 89
Plemons, Icy 139, 140, 141
Pollak, Lisa 8, 136
Porterdale, GA 48, 49
Pruett, Bill 134, 135

R

Reynolds, Burt 40
Rivers, Ed 27
Roosevelt, President Franklin D. 101, 103, 168
Rucker, John 45
Ruckersville, GA 43, 45

S

Salter, Chuck 47, 136, 138, 175
Salter, J.D. 164
Salter, Sallye Roberts 175
Sams, Anita 8, 15
Savannah, GA 45, 79, 80, 81, 83, 84, 112, 114, 123
Schlatterville, GA 53
Sherman's, General William T. 91, 92
Sinkwich, Frank 169
Spring Place, GA 145, 147
Stephens, William 80
Stradivari, Antonio 25
Sugar Valley, GA 60, 61
Sullivan, Charlotte 69, 70, 71
Sullivan, Reverend J.N. 89, 90
Summerour, Joseph "Jay" 75, 76, 77, 78
Sylvia the Ghost 109, 110, 111

T

Talmadge, Gene 27
Talmadge, Herman 27

Tichenor, Emily 15
Tichenor, Henry McDaniel 15
Tombs, General Robert 16
Trail of Tears 75
Trammell, Amy 35, 37
Trammell, Bill 35, 37
Trippi, Charley 169
Tucker, Reverend Dan 122, 123, 124
Turners Corner, GA 63

V

Valentino, Rudolph 69, 71
Vann, James 145, 147, 148
Voigt, Fred 51, 52, 53

W

Walker, W.W. "Wink" 110, 111
Wares Crossroads, GA 38
Ware, William "Pete" 38, 40
Warfield, Frances 15
Warner Robins 9, 104, 108
Waycross, GA 10, 51, 53, 54, 144, 175
West, Mae 70
Wheeler, Wallace 21
White, John 45
Whitlock, GA 142
Wiley, Hugh 54, 55
Williams, Jim 114, 115
Williford, Robert L. 122, 123, 124
Wingate, Jack 7, 149
Wyatt, Frances 169

About the Author

Charles E. Salter was born in Ocilla, Georgia, June 9, 1933, and lived in Greensboro, Athens and Waycross before attending the University of Georgia, where he received a degree in journalism. He began his newspaper career as a reporter for the *Macon News* in Macon, Georgia. He was a reporter, wire editor and fishing columnist there before joining the *Atlanta Journal* in 1967.

During thirty-one years at the *Journal*, Salter worked as a copy editor, makeup editor, picture editor and weather columnist, and for twenty-four years he wrote fishing columns and features for the afternoon paper and the Sunday editions of the *Atlanta Journal and Constitution*. From 1976 to 1980, Salter traveled the state, writing the "Georgia Rambler" column.

His wife, Sallye Roberts Salter, also a UGA graduate, was a reporter for the *Macon News* as well and covered commercial real estate and development for the *Atlanta Constitution* for thirty-one years.

Salter and his wife are retired and live in Atlanta. They have three children—Suzanne Alexander of Thomasville, Georgia, Laura Braaten of Cazenovia, New York, and Charles E. "Chuck" Salter Jr. of New York, New York—and five grandchildren.

Salter is the author of a book on fishing, *Bent Poles and Tight Lines*, published in 1982.

Visit us at
www.historypress.net